Elizabeth Williams Champney

Three Vassar Girls abroad

Rambles of three College Girls on a Vacation Trip through France and Spain for

Amusement and Instruction

Elizabeth Williams Champney

Three Vassar Girls abroad
Rambles of three College Girls on a Vacation Trip through France and Spain for Amusement and Instruction

ISBN/EAN: 9783337148294

Printed in Europe, USA, Canada, Australia, Japan

Cover: Foto ©Andreas Hilbeck / pixelio.de

More available books at **www.hansebooks.com**

ON THE LAKE AT VASSAR.

RAMBLES OF THREE COLLEGE GIRLS ON A VACATION TRIP THROUGH FRANCE AND SPAIN FOR AMUSEMENT AND INSTRUCTION.

WITH THEIR HAPS AND MISHAPS.

BY

LIZZIE W. CHAMPNEY,

AUTHOR OF "A NEGLECTED CORNER OF EUROPE," ETC.

WITH NEARLY A HUNDRED AND FIFTY ORIGINAL ILLUSTRATIONS BY "CHAMP"
(J. WELLS CHAMPNEY) AND OTHER DISTINGUISHED ARTISTS.

BOSTON:
ESTES AND LAURIAT.
1883.

Copyright, 1882,
BY ESTES AND LAURIAT.

All Rights Reseved.

CONTENTS.

		PAGE
I.	PARIS	15
II.	FRENCH SOCIETY	36
III.	JOAN OF ARC'S TOWN	56
IV.	AN HISTORIC CHATEAU	70
V.	OCEAN AND MOUNTAINS	80
VI.	MADRID	92
VII.	THE DEVOTIONAL IMAGES OF SPAIN	100
VIII.	TOLEDO	108
IX.	CORDOVA AND THE CALIPHATE	118
X.	SEVILLE	127
XI.	GRANADA	134
XII.	A BOUQUET OF LEGENDS	150
XIII.	LISBON AND CINTRA	182
XIV.	THE NORTH OF PORTUGAL	199
XV.	A GLIMPSE AT AFRICA	216
XVI.	HOME AGAIN	229

ILLUSTRATIONS.

	PAGE
On the Lake at Vassar . *Frontispiece.*	
Through the Gorge	14
The Grand Opera House . . .	17
"As she sat on a Grassy Hillside" .	21
The Sainte Chapelle	22
Palais de L'Élysée	23
Porte St. Denis	27
"Which of the Three?" . . .	28
Palace of the Luxembourg . . .	29
The Observatory	30
Dome des Invalides	33
Hotel de Cluny	37
The Donjon of Vincennes . . .	38
"Not in Need of a Porter" . .	40
Cabinet de Verdure	41
Labyrinth of Versailles . . .	45
On the Train	47
Chateau de Fontainebleau (View Taken from the Garden) . . .	50
Papa Le Prince and Cecilia . .	51
Chateau de Fontainebleau (the Oval Court)	54
Chateau de Maintenon . . .	57
View of Chartres	59
Joan in Prison	61
Fifine as Bonne	64
The Baroness's Cousin . . .	66
Chateau du Moutier	67
Chateau de Blois, East Side . .	70
Chateau de Blois, from the North .	71
Murder of the Duc de Guise . .	75
A Window	79
A Leaf from Maud's Sketch Book .	81
Making a Picture Herself . . .	83

	PAGE
On Muleback	84
Death of Roland	85
Pepita	88
Charlemagne's School of the Palace .	89
Studying Velasquez . . .	94
The Library of the Escorial . .	97
The Courier Explains . . .	99
Nuestra Señora de Guadalupe . .	100
Nuestra Señora del Pilar . .	101
Nuestra Señora de Monserrat . .	103
Nuestra Señora de La Merced . .	105
Nuestra Señora de Toledo . .	105
Nuestra Señora d'Atocha . .	106
Nuestra Señora de los Desemparados .	106
Nuestra Señora de Carmen . .	107
A Street in Toledo	109
Interior Court at Toledo . .	112
Interior of the Cathedral at Toledo .	113
Cardinal Ximenes	115
Annie Laurie	119
Father St. Iago Matamoras . .	125
A Murillo Altar Boy . . .	129
The Giralda	130
He Calls this an Artistic Creation .	131
Patio de la Alberca	135
Charles V.	139
Fortuny's Model	141
A Child's Funeral	144
Looking over the Photographs . .	145
The Generalife	147
Tomb of Runjeet Sing . . .	151
Aladdin's Gate	155
Palace of Copal Bhowan . . .	158
Pagoda of Chillambaran . . .	159

ILLUSTRATIONS.

	PAGE
Garden Gate of the Taj	163
Interior Court, Tanjore	169
Mausoleum, Golconda	173
Mosque, Triplican	177
Fish Boy of Lisbon	183
Lord Gubbins	186
Castle of Penha de Cintra	191
Donkey Boy at Cintra	194
Mafra	195
Beggar	197
Peasant Woman and Donkey	198
View of Oporto	201
A Leaf from Maud's Sketch Book	203
"Beggars Might Ride"	204
Ox Cart	205
Cathedral of Guimarães	207
The Castle of Guimarães	210
Gateway	214
Rock of Gibraltar	217
Sketch in Gibraltar	219
Bazaar in Tunis	221
A Santo	223
Door of the Mosque of Bou Médina	225
Home at Last	232
The Envelope	232

THREE VASSAR GIRLS ABROAD.

THREE VASSAR GIRLS ABROAD.

CHAPTER I.

PARIS.

THEY were three Vassar girls; Cecilia Boylston, Maud Van Vechten, and Barbara Atchison. They had moored their boat under the willows, and while other girls improved their hour of exercise by quick pulling up and down the pond, they discussed an important project in the privacy of their green-canopied, water-paved arbor. Vacation was approaching, and plans for the summer were now the absorbing topics of conversation. Maud sat in the stern, her pretty face silhouetted darkly against the radiant disc of a Japanese umbrella, which, with the sunlight filtering through, had all the effect of a rose-window. It was she who had called her two dearest friends to secret conclave to inform them that her arrangements were happily settled. She was to go to Europe with her sister, Mrs. Arnold, who proposed to spend the summer in travel, and to meet her husband, a naval officer, at Nice, in the winter.

"I shall have to come back alone in the fall," said Maud, "for I would not fall out of our class for anything, and you know we'll be Juniors next year. Sister says there are always people returning from Europe in the fall, and she can easily find company for me."

"I think you are the luckiest girl in the world, Maud," exclaimed Barbara Atchison; "here am I, with a lot of money, and nowhere to go. Father is stationed in the Black Hills, this summer, and he doesn't want me out there. He writes, 'You have seen enough of Western society for the present. You are too old to be kept in the background as a child, and too young to do the honors of my house. If your mother had lived, home would have been the best place for you; as it is, I wish you to profit by the civilizing influences of the East. You write enthusiastically of your New York friend; visit with her, this summer, and I will pay all expenses.' There it is, and my New York friend is going to Europe."

"Why not come with me, Barb?"

"Elegant! But would your sister take charge of such a harum-scarum thing as I am, a western officer's daughter, who has been brought up on the Plains and in forts? And is there time to write to Papa?"

"Yes, yes, of course she would; and there's plenty of time. And, oh, Saint, won't you come too?"

Saint was Cecilia's pet name.

"I intended to go to Munich and continue my music, after we graduate," she replied, "and I would enjoy this summer trip immensely, but I am afraid I can't afford it."

"Now, Saint, just look here!" exclaimed Barbara. "If we go without you, there will be three of us, a dreadfully odd number. We will have to pay just as much for carriages and rooms as if there were four; and I will have to room alone, which I detest. If you go, it will cheapen everything, and I insist on paying just what I would have to if you were not in the party. That will bring down your expenses somewhat. Then you are the only one of us that can speak French creditably. We need you, my dear, as interpreter. And what an improving influence you will have over me! When Papa hears that I am going abroad with a clergyman's daughter from Boston, he will believe that the civilizing influences have begun in good earnest."

THE GRAND OPERA HOUSE.

"It would be delightful," mused St. Cecilia. "I wonder whether I would have to buy a very expensive outfit in the way of clothes."

"I shall get everything over there," replied Maud. "Sister Lily manages to go abroad at least every three years, so as to do all our shopping in Paris. Dresses are a bother while one is travelling, and you have a first-rate tourist's wardrobe; that Boston waterproof of yours will have occasion to flap its wings and crow over all our finery."

The girls laughed at this allusion to Saint's waterproof, for it was a very characteristic bit of costume. Barbara declared that it completed the mediævalism of her name, giving her the appearance of a nun, or a saint, in flowing gown of sackcloth.

"You are not going to Germany. I shouldn't mind that, for I would like to see a little of other parts of Europe," said St. Cecilia, "and I'm almost sure of Germany after I graduate. I daresay, too, that I can enjoy many musical advantages in France and Spain. There is the Grand Opera to begin with."

"Yes, and think, Saint, there are cathedrals, and stained glass, and old masters! Dear me! I don't see how you can hesitate for a moment."

And Saint did not hesitate long. A favorable letter came from the Rev. Mr. Boylston, and early in July the three merry maids looked out from their windows at the Hotel de Louvre, at the imposing pile opposite. "I am so glad," said Maud, "that Lily chose the Hotel de Louvre, for now we have but to cross the street to reach the galleries, and I expect to spend most of my time while in Paris there. Think of the art treasures! Girls, the Venus of Milo is in that lower gallery of sculpture. Raphael's Belle Jardinière, Da Vinci's Holy Family, Veronese's Marriage of Cana, Murillo's Immaculate Conception, Titian's Entombment! Then there is the Rubens Gallery, and the long array of French painters that we know so well by reputation. I shall take my sketch-box over and paint every morning."

"Now, Maud," interrupted Mrs. Arnold, "this trip was for pleasure, you know, not work. There are the parks and the theatres, the shops and society. We have only two weeks for Paris, and we must make the most of our opportunities."

"I will do what you choose, sister, in the afternoon and evening, but every morning I shall reserve for the Louvre Galleries. I must carry away a few souvenirs of the treasures which it contains."

Their first evening was spent at the Grand Opera. This was almost as great a delight to the other girls as to Cecilia, for, while she revelled in the music and was oblivious to all outward things, Maud's artistic eye gained keen delight from Baudry's frescoes in the *foyer* or promenade hall, and from the superb architectural effects of the exterior. Barbara too, who had a somewhat crude love for obvious magnificence, gloated over the general effect. "Now this is what I call a palace," she said, as she stood before the grand staircase. "I don't believe the Grand Monarque ever dreamed of such gorgeousness. Positively, it is so beautiful that it makes one forget to look at the ladies' dresses." This was the summit of effect for Barbara, whose love for display in dress was so barbarian that the girls sometimes said that she was rightly named. In reality, Barbara's startling costumes were only experiments in search of the beautiful. She had not inherited fine taste, or been brought up to walk between the strait hedgerows of artistic requirements like Maud, and she knew nothing of the culture and philosophy which had shaped Cecilia's life. Her nature was groping blindly, like a wild vine reaching out eager tendrils towards some high object of aspiration. Everything heroic and noble elicited her admiration, and her heart was as tender as it was true.

The party made an excursion one day to Ecouen, as Maud wished to visit the studios of the artist colony there. Barbara was as enthusiastic as any of the party over the gentle-faced mothers and sweet children in Frere's *genre* pictures, and over all the varying styles of the younger artists who have clustered around this great man. But she knew that she was admiring a talent in which she had no part; and as she sat on a grassy hillside under the old Chateau of Montmorency, looking away over the fresh country landscape to the spires and domes of Paris, she thought to herself, "How satisfying it must be to have a purpose in life like Maud's, to be an artist or a musician like Saint. Now I have no specialty, no particular talent. Perhaps I will find one during this tour." A bit of a poem by George Herbert occurred to her and she breathed it as a prayer:

> "Lord, place me in Thy concert,
> Give one note to my poor reed."

Barbara often accompanied Saint in her ecclesiological pilgrimages, and puzzled her brain, vainly attempting to trace different styles of architecture. St. Cecilia had a passion for churches. The one she loved in Paris, second only to Nôtre Dame, was the Sainte Chapelle. It is a dainty, graceful building, with arrowy spire, and many pinnacles pointing their silent fingers upward. It has been called "the completest specimen of the religious architecture of the middle of the thirteenth century." It was built by St. Louis to receive the relics which he brought from the Holy

"AS SHE SAT ON A GRASSY HILLSIDE."

Land, and is hardly more than a beautifully chased and ornamented reliquary. The Cathedral of Nôtre Dame was more impressive, and Cecilia, who was familiar with Victor Hugo's novels, felt, when she reached it, that she had met with an old friend. Its superb flying buttresses, its rainbow windows, the two great towers with their quaint gargoyles and clashing bells, the rose windows like a rosette of jewels on the breast of a general, the awe-inspiring aisles and the uplifting music of the organs were all as familiar as though she had known them long ago. The cathedral stands on the island of La Cité, in the middle of the Seine, which in turn divides Paris the old from Paris the new. On the left bank of the Seine is the Latin Quarter, with its old universities, crooked and narrow streets, and time-blackened houses. It is the Paris of which Eugène Sue and the older dramatists and novelists wrote, and has all the mouldy flavor of ancient times.

THE SAINTE CHAPELLE.

On the right is the gay sparkling Paris of the present, with its wide boulevards, enticing shops, resplendent palaces, and superb parks.

PALAIS DE L'ÉLYSÉE.

Mrs. Arnold could not understand how her sister could immure herself in a picture gallery, or Cecilia go prowling about in churches when the avenues presented such a merry out-of-door panorama of sunshine and color. Every afternoon she whirled them away in an open carriage through the Champs Elysées, past the Palais de l'Industrie, and the more interesting Palace de l'Elysée, once the fascinating residence of that most fascinating of women, Madame Pompadour, under the Arc de Triomphe to the Bois de Boulogne. Mrs. Arnold, though their senior, was far more frivolous than any one of the girls. She was a living proof of the absurdity of a chaperone for earnest American girls. Though she had visited France several times she spoke the language poorly, and was apt to lose her head as to locality or the exigencies of any sudden emergency. It was Saint who made inquiries of the officials and acted as general interpreter for the party. It was Barbara who consulted the map in the guide-book and led them straight through puzzling labyrinths to their desired destinations, and it was Maud who settled every point of social etiquette. Most frequently the decision came in the shape of a firm refusal. "We have not time, sister; if we were intending to remain a year or more, we might go into society, but as it is we cannot afford it."

Mrs. Arnold was not, however, an easy person to thwart. She had numerous old friends in Paris with whom she exchanged courtesies, and she managed to convoy the girls to a number of evening receptions. There was a certain Madame Le Prince, connected in some way with the displaced nobility, who held salon in a fashionable quarter in Paris, to whose rooms she did not for some time succeed in enticing Maud, for Mrs. Arnold had unguardedly remarked that Madame Le Prince was looking for a *parti* for her son, a young gentleman reduced by adverse circumstances to a commercial career, but who might, by a turn in the governmental machinery, mount to a title. Maud had taken alarm at once.

"I will not be bartered for a title," she asserted, "and wild horses shall not drag me to Madame Le Prince's soirees."

"No one wishes to barter you, my dear," replied Mrs. Arnold coolly, "and I am sure it shows considerable self-complacency on your part to take it for granted that Madame Le Prince will desire you as a daughter-in-law."

"She does not desire me or any particular young girl. What she wishes is a dowry — some young woman who shall bring her son a sufficient fortune to enable him to go out of trade and wait with dignity an elevation of rank which will probably never come. If you do not wish to suggest me or one of the other girls for that situation, our being there will look as if you did, and we shall be the talk of the American colony."

"Don't get angry, Maud," replied Mrs. Arnold; "it makes your face red, and you have enough of that color in your hair. I can go to Madame Le Prince's without you, and we will not refer again to the subject."

But she did refer to it again, most emphatically, as after chapters will show.

Barbara was as delighted as a child with all that she was. She indulged in suppressed screams of delight at each new wonder, while Cecilia observed everything with a conscientious interest which seemed to consider it a duty to lose nothing and to mark that which was good, and a calm discrimination which brought everything up for judgment before the highest standards.

Maud was only interested in art. Everything else bored her, as she considered it so much time lost from her favorite pursuit.

Barbara took a vivid delight in out-of-door Paris. She loved to linger in the Champs Élysées, and watch the delight of the children in the Theatre Guignol, the French Punch-and-Judy show. It seemed to her that the great obelisk in the Place de la Concorde could tell her many a legend if it cared, to do so, and she made it a little speech concerning its huge brother in Central Park, for there seemed something pathetic to her in the way they had wandered away from sunny Egypt to be so far separated in the end. Enchanting Parc Monceaux, with its glancing fountains and curious

PORTE ST. DENIS.

grottoes, was, perhaps, her favorite resort, but she had an infinite respect for all the historical monuments which Cecilia explained to her; the Porte St. Denis which commemorates the victories of Louis XIV. in the Netherlands; the Column which marks the place of the Bastile, and the Column Vendome which celebrates Napoleon's victories. Barbara had been specially commissioned by her father to look up all memorials of Napoleon. She kept putting the duty off, as the days whirled by, making meagre notes now and then of his coronation at Notre Dame, of the Column Vendome, and of such chance scraps as came in her way. "When we go out to Versailles," Maud assured her, "you will find no end of historical pictures which will celebrate every event in his career."

One afternoon, when the three girls were together in the Champs Élysées, Barbara called Maud's attention to a melancholy individual seated in a drooping attitude upon one of the benches. "He is my ghost," she said. "Wherever I go, I see that dejected and unhappy man. I am sure that he is an American and dreadfully homesick. Whatever brought him to Europe I can't imagine."

WHICH OF THE THREE?

"I meet him frequently, too," remarked Saint.

"And I," added Maud. "I believe, from the crape around his hat, that he is a widower, and that he is deeply absorbed in contemplating which of us girls he will take."

The other girls laughed heartily in spite of the absurdity of the idea, and the innocent old man became the theme of much sport.

One pleasant day, the three girls set out for the Latin Quarter together. Maud carried her Japanese parasol and sketch-box, which made her quite as marked a figure as St. Cecilia in her waterproof and near-sighted glasses, and Barbara, as was usual on such occasions, was armed with a vermilion-bound guide-book. The guide-book Barbara insisted on carrying everywhere, even into churches, much to Saint's annoyance, who suggested one day that Barbara might at least respect people's feelings sufficiently to have her beloved Baedeker bound as a Bible or prayer-book.

On this occasion, the girls had each a special point in view, but had agreed to do all three in company. Cecilia wished to hear the Stabat Mater at St. Sulpice, and Barbara and Maud duly accompanied

PALACE OF THE LUXEMBOURG.

her, though the former could not resist sly peeps into her guide-book, and Maud made a surreptitious sketch of a Madonna which hung over one of the side altars. When they came out they all paused before the imposing fountain in front of the church.

"It says," said Barbara, who always referred thus to her guide, "that these statues represent the four most celebrated preachers in France, Bossuet, Fenelon, Massillon, and Fléchier."

"I wonder why they placed them guard over a fountain?" Maud queried, carelessly.

"Why, I think it very appropriate," replied Barbara, seriously; "they were such great spouters, you know."

THE OBSERVATORY.

"Barb, Barb, you are too bad," groaned Saint.

"Barb is like a fountain herself," laughed Maud; "you can't keep her from gushing. What are you girls going to do while I begin my study in the Luxembourg?"

"We will wander about in that lovely garden," replied Barbara.

They strolled along the terrace among the statues of women

celebrated in the history of France, and tried to guess how Marie de Medicis felt when she saw the building completed according to her wish. Veterans were sunning themselves on benches beside the wall, and pretty children were sporting among the roses and carnations of the garden. Suddenly Saint noticed a dome-crowned building at the end of one of the avenues. "I do believe, Barb," she exclaimed, "that that is the observatory."

"How lucky that I brought my Baedeker," murmured Barbara, as she opened the guide-book, and proceeded, still walking, to consult it. "Yes, it is the observatory; do you want to visit it?"

"Yes, indeed, if they will let us."

"We can at least try."

But the little grille or iron gate was fast locked, and the portress refused to open it unless the demoiselles would bring papers signed by prominent officials.

Saint looked through the bars longingly. "I wonder which is the ball-room," she remarked, musingly.

"The ball-room!" exclaimed Barbara, interested at once.

"Why, yes. Have you never heard that story? When Miss Mitchell was in France the celebrated French astronomer, Leverrier, invited her to spend an evening at the observatory. Professor Mitchell went in a simple suit of Quaker gray. When she arrived she was ushered into a brilliantly-lighted ball-room. Leverrier had given a ball in her honor, and there were the noblesse of France in full evening costume — trains, lace, low necks and diamonds — assembled to receive her."

Intense admiration shone in Barbara's eyes. "How cheap all their tinsel finery must have looked beside our star," she exclaimed enthusiastically. "There is a woman who has made something really grand of her life. Full dress, indeed! The presumption of expecting her to attend a court ball."

"I thought it absurd enough, but that is the French way. In

England, when they wish to do honor to a scientist, they give a dinner instead. I am sure I don't know which I should dread most, a dinner at Oxford or a ball at the French Observatory."

"Dinners are poky things," remarked Barbara. "I'd choose the ball."

"That is because we Americans resemble the French more than we do the English."

They returned to Maud, who was still diligently painting.

She closed her sketch-box as she saw them approaching. "I can come here some other day," she said, generously. "I had just as lief my study should dry before I go at it again; and if we do not leave immediately we will never get around to Barb's point of interest, the Hôtel des Invalides."

"I am sure I am interested in everything," replied Barbara, with truth, "and I never should have thought of poking round after those old Invalides if it had not been for father."

The Hôtel des Invalides, however, proved more interesting than they had anticipated. The tattered flags that chronicled Napoleon's victories seemed to droop sadly over his tomb, and the old veterans so cozily established in the comfortable hotel recalled to their minds those who had followed the great general in his campaigns, and who never would believe that he was dead. Their little gardens with child-play of fortifications and battle-field were interesting and touching as well. One veteran had arranged his in imitation of the Rock at St. Helena, with a little lead image of the man in the "*redingote grise*," the heavy gray overcoat which was characteristic of the first Napoleon. There had been men in the institution, so their guide said, who had wounds for nearly every one of Napoleon's great campaigns, a star-shaped, powder-blackened scar in the cheek, received in Italy,— of which the owner was as proud as of a medal of honor; an eye destroyed by scorching desert sands at the time of the battle of the Pyramids; a sabre cut on the arm at Austerlitz; four fingers frozen on

DOME DES INVALIDES.

the march back from Moscow; a wound in the leg, the most trifling of all, but the one that rankled most, received at Waterloo.

Barbara's letter, when it went to her father, was not a cold statement of facts and dates, but a vivid and enthusiastic sketch of the career of the great conqueror.

She was beginning the study of history in a new way, not by dry dates and names, but from monuments of heroic or brilliant deeds and souvenirs of touching episodes. The great book lay open before her. She had read but one leaf, and henceforward she was an insatiable student. Other characters kept coming up as centres of interest, their lives overlapping and interlacing, making the most romantic and fascinating of continued stories. "I shall read and read," she said to herself, "and perhaps, by and by, I shall find out what to do with my own little life."

CHAPTER II.

FRENCH SOCIETY.

"WHERE are you going to paint to-day, Maud?" Barbara asked one morning, in their second week in Paris, as she saw Maud preparing her sketch-box for an expedition; "I hope not in that tiresome Louvre."

"No, I am going to the Cluny palace."

"Where is that? Has it anything to do with Cluny lace?"

"It is in the Latin quarter, and is used nowadays as a museum of antiquities; it is filled with the most delightful old rubbish. Among other things, I believe there is some splendid lace. Come with me, and you will enjoy rummaging among the antique furniture, tapestries, carvings, vestments, porcelains, and all manner of bric-a-brac."

"Oh! I don't know; I'm rather tired of museums. They stretch away off to infinity, and you are always congratulating yourself that you have reached the last gallery, when another, with a slippery wax floor piled with loads of fascinating things which you haven't the moral courage to resist, is suddenly sprung upon you."

"But the Hotel Cluny is not such a vast and dreary monument. The beauty of it is that it is little and cosy enough to make a nice dwelling-house."

"What are you going to paint? Are there rows and rows of pictures to copy? If there are, I declare I'll not go. My brain just swims when I attempt to disentangle the pictures I've seen in Paris."

"No, there are only a few delightfully absurd old pre-Raphaelite things that will make you laugh heartily. It is just the quaintest, dearest old house in the world, a bit of medieval times brought to life again. It would be very easy to imagine that the 'Reine Blanche,' the widow of Louis XII., had just left her bed-room, and we had slipped in by some magic. The carved state bed with its canopy and faded velvet hangings are all there, just as in the olden time. I am

HOTEL DE CLUNY.

going to paint an interior, a carved fire-place, which one sees looking out from that bed-room."

"Well, I'll go with you, Maud, for I must choose between that and the excursion which Saint makes out to the Donjon of Vincennes. The churches are dreary enough sometimes, and I know I could not stand a prison."

"Is Saint going alone?"

"No, those wofully tedious friends of hers, the Shawmuts, invited her. They want her to go with them, too, to the Abbey of St. Denis. They seem to have come to France on purpose to find all the gloomy and repulsive places. The very look of the photograph of the Donjon

THE DONJON OF VINCENNES.

of Vincennes was enough to frighten me from going there. Mrs. Shawmut was telling, too, a tragic story of the assassination of the Duc d' Enghien, which occurred there. I am sure I should see the young man's ghost in every shadowy corner."

"I am not sure but you would find the excursion an entertaining one. I remember Dumas made the place vividly real to me in his Trois Mousquetaires."

"Indeed, I am not sorry I came here instead of going to the dungeon," Barbara exclaimed, as they mounted the curious staircase of the Hotel Cluny, and entered the armor-hung hall; "it is just the place for an adventure of some sort. There is an assassin behind that tapestry, I am morally certain, and if we wait until dusk, a ghost will glide across that gallery. There are blood-stains yonder on the polished oak floor, and Borgia poisons in those old Venetian glasses. — Dear, dear, it is just too lovely for anything."

"It is the best place in Paris to paint a medieval interior," replied Maud, practically planting her easel and camp-stool, and opening her box of colors. "Don't feel obliged to sit here beside me all the time, but explore the building and see if you can discover a mystery."

Barbara wandered away, inspecting the illuminated missals and old ivories displayed behind the glass doors of the cabinets, and falling into a trance of mingled admiration and amazement before some Palissy plaques filled with porcelain eels and craw-fish, the like of which she had never seen before. She returned after a time to Maud, and the two girls descended the spiral staircase, and lunched in the court, seated among specimens of antique sculpture, relics of old Roman days, following Cæsar's conquest of Gaul.

Maud ran up stairs to pack her artist furniture, the light would be different in the afternoon, and Barbara waited for her in the garden. Presently she heard her approaching and speaking to some one. Turning she saw Maud looking back indignantly at a young Frenchman; evidently her remarks were not encouraging, for he waved his hand apologetically, and retreated.

"What was he saying to you?" Barbara asked with much interest.

"The impudent thing wanted to carry my box for me."

"And what did you say?"

"I told him I was not in need of a porter."

"Good, he must have felt complimented. I hope he thought you really took him for one."

"It is the first time any one has ever spoken to me in Paris. I am so vexed because it helps demonstrate Sister's theory, that girls should not go out without a chaperone."

"I think you managed him very nicely. I suppose he thought all American girls were like Daisy Miller, and had never heard the proverb, — There are two kinds of girls, girls who flirt, and girls who go to Vassar College."

"Very likely the benighted individual

NOT IN NEED OF A PORTER

never heard of Vassar." (A supposition which was afterwards proved to be the fact.)

"But Maud, about the chaperone business. If I had been with you I don't see why I would not have answered just as well as your sister."

CABINET DE VERDURE.

"You are not a married lady."

"How is anybody to know that? I am taller than Mrs. Arnold, and have loads more dignity. The next time we go out together, I'll wear my diamond ear-rings. Only married ladies in France wear diamonds. Then I would like to see anybody dare speak to us."

"You had better borrow Saint's spectacles. What we need is some old-looking person. As you say Sister is no better than one of us. She's prettier and flightier than we are. I am sure I always feel that I am chaperoning her when we are together. Saint has never been molested, and she has been to nearly all the churches in Paris alone."

"Which proves to my mind that well-conducted, earnest American girls do not need a chaperone, especially when there are two or three of us together."

"We will know better after this trip is over, but if I ever come to Europe again, and have to bring a dragon, I will bring an older and a more sensible one than Sister."

The next day was one long to be remembered. It was spent at Versailles. The four wandered together through the miles of historical paintings, peeped almost awe-stricken into the rooms once occupied by the unfortunate Louis XVI. and his lovely Queen, Marie Antoinette, shivered a little at the glassy coldness of the Mirror Salon, and descended with a long drawn breath of relief to the gardens, among the most charming in all Europe. The box and yews were cut into fantastic forms; there were long avenues and *parterres* of brilliant flowers, terraces of imposing stairs, statues, and, above all, fountains. It was a day *des grandes eaux*. "The Queen of the Frogs" was showering the thirsty stone turtles, in another fountain mischievous little Cupids were blowing water at each other through carved billows, and the startled attitude of the statues of the horses in the Rocher of Apollo, that seemed to have been led to one of the pools to drink, was explained by the splashing and leaping water about them. They lingered after dusk until the stars came out, as did nearly all the visitors that evening, for there was to be an illumination. The grand fountain of all, "The Triumph of Neptune," spouted its many columns into the night air, while all around Bengal lights were burning, and their various colors, crimson, blue, yellow and emerald, were reflected in the jets of water with all the changing brilliancy of prisms.

"Now I understand," said Barbara, "why Paris received its name. The word is a contraction, only three letters dropped out of Par(a-d)is(e)."

They reached their hotel tired out but enthusiastic. "It is certainly the most interesting day and brilliant evening we have spent so far," said Maud. "Those fountains were simply unpaintable, they were geysers of splintered rainbows."

"There is one more excursion which we must make before we leave Paris," said Mrs. Arnold, carelessly, "and that is to Fontainebleau. It would never do to miss the palace, and you know, Maud, that the artist colony of Barbizon is on the edge of the park."

"Yes," replied Maud," I would like to go to Barbizon, since we have seen the other artistic colony at Ecouen."

"My dear," said Mrs. Arnold with a trace of triumph in her voice, "you shall go to both. We will set out for Fontainebleau to-morrow. Madame Le Prince has a villa on the confines of the forest. She has invited us out to spend the night with her, and the next day in exploring the palace. Monsieur Le Prince is quite a historian; he will be an excellent guide in that great rambling caravansary."

Maud's face was not encouraging, but she had already committed herself to a desire to visit the palace, and her sister followed up her advantage.

"You can have no objection to going, for Armand is not at home, he is in business somewhere near Marseilles. You will see only two

VERSAILLES.

old people who have been very polite to me, and to refuse whose kind invitation would be rudeness indeed."

The next day the four girls, for Mrs. Arnold was herself very young and childish in appearance, took the train for Fontainebleau.

They congratulated themselves on securing an entire compartment, but just as they rolled out of the station, a young man sprang hastily in. Barbara grasped Maud's hand impulsively, it was the very forward person whom they had met at the Hotel Cluny. He seemed in no way abashed by the *rencontre*, but made a thousand polite apologies for intruding upon an apartment which he had not the time to notice was reserved for ladies. Mrs. Arnold bowed very prettily and smiled, but the girls retreated with freezing hauteur behind their thick travelling veils. Mrs. Arnold, to make up for this lack of cordiality, attempted to converse with the stranger in broken English. As she was not proficient in French, she always spoke to foreigners in as close an imitation as possible of their own efforts in English. It seemed to her that they must understand it better than the language itself, pure and simple.

ON THE TRAIN.

"Do not derange yourself, Monsieur," said Mrs. Arnold, sweetly. "*Il ne faut pas apologize.*"

"Do be still, Lily," whispered Maud, in an agony of despair, "that is the insufferable person who spoke to us at the Cluny."

Mrs. Arnold's manner underwent a sudden change, she remembered the responsibility of her position, and at once assumed a majestic and freezing attitude. The young gentleman made no remark, and was evidently quite as uncomfortable as they were. Arrived at the station, they found an open carriage sent by Madame Le Prince, waiting for them. They had hardly taken their places, however, when, to their utter amazement, the young man mounted to a seat beside the driver. Mrs. Arnold addressed the coachman in broken English, and demanded that their fellow-voyager should be required to descend. The man stared at her in dumb astonishment, not comprehending her meaning. "Translate for me, Saint," Mrs. Arnold insisted, and Cecilia politely, and in perfectly good French, intimated that this was not a public carriage. The young man looked up with a merry expression. "It is true," he said. "A thousand pardons," and touching his hat gracefully, he clambered down.

"Dear me," murmured Mrs. Arnold, "I never heard of such presumption. Don't talk to me about girls travelling without the protection of a married lady, it is utterly out of the question."

"Mrs. Arnold!" exclaimed Barbara, "that objectionable young man has taken a cab, and is actually following us."

"He is indeed," said Maud, who had ventured one sidelong glance backward. "Oh! how shall we ever get rid of him?"

"He will stop somewhere in the town," said Saint, composedly. "I am quite sure that he is not really following us, but that his way and ours happens to lie in the same direction."

"I should say it did," replied Barbara, "we have passed the town, and he still keeps on the even tenor and soprano of his way."

"He will desist in the pursuit when we enter the park gates of the Le Prince estate," said Mrs. Arnold, confidently. But to their chagrin, the cab passed the gate-lodge just behind them, and followed them up the avenue.

"How very mortifying," said Mrs. Arnold. "What will Madame Le Prince think of us? He must be intoxicated."

They mounted the steps and rang the bell. While waiting for a response, their follower alighted, joined them, and threw open the great door with a courteous " *Entrez, Mesdames.*"

"Sir," exclaimed Mrs. Arnold in her most withering manner, " this is not a public house."

" True," he replied, with the same merry twinkle in his eye, " but it is my father's house, to which you are very welcome."

It was Mrs. Arnold's turn to be nonplussed, this was the young M. Armand Le Prince of whom his mother had so often spoken. The girls, too, were much confused, but the young man's merriment was contagious, and a hearty laugh helped them over the embarrassment of the situation. Papa Le Prince, a fat, white-haired, old gentleman, dressed entirely in white linen, and Madame, also fat and white-haired, but clad conventionally in black silk, gave them a most cordial welcome, and the evening passed very pleasantly.

Early the next morning they set out together to view the Palace of Fontainebleau. Their way led them through the famous park so celebrated in the history of France. They reached at length the quaint jumble of incongrous buildings which makes up the palace. It seemed to Saint as if it were a living thing, some wonderful century-plant originally set out by Robert the Pious, and nursed and tended by Louis VII. and Philippe Auguste, under whose reign, and that of Louis IX., it had put out various stalks and branches; while in that of Francis I., it had blossomed into a splendid hall, and unlike other plants, had kept its first flower while other buds and blossoms gathered about it under Henry IV., Louis Philippe, and Napoleon III. Papa Le Prince knew every legend of love and crime connected with the place, and without him they never could have found their way through the maze of galleries, grand and spiral staircases, secret pasages, suites of salons, mysterious chambers concealed in the walls, haunted corridors, sightly towers, and frescoed halls. Papa Le Prince led the way, escorting St. Cecilia, Madame followed with Mrs. Arnold and

Maud on either hand, and Barbara and young Monsieur Armand brought up the rear. Papa Le Prince admired Cecilia greatly. "What a holy woman!" he remarked to Mrs. Arnold, "she has evidently been brought up in a convent. She cares for nothing but churches and sacred music. She is doubtless destined for a nun-

CHATEAU DE FONTAINEBLEAU (VIEW TAKEN FROM THE GARDEN).

nery!" In their out of door rambles, Papa Le Prince carried an immense white umbrella lined with green, with which he gallantly shaded Cecilia, insisting on carrying her waterproof upon his other arm. They got along very well together, for Cecilia admired his genuine kindliness of heart, and Papa Le Prince was determined to contribute toward giving her as much enjoyment as possible before

PAPA LE PRINCE AND CECILIA

she entered upon a religious life. Barbara and her escort also soon became quite confidential. They chatted together in French, which Barbara used rather lamely.

"Did you know who Maud was when you spoke to her at the Cluny?" Barbara asked.

"Not at all. I saw that she was an American, and very pretty. My mother had written me a great deal of Miss Maud Van Vechten, but I imagined that she was very homely, and that I should detest her."

"Why did you think that?"

"Because my mother wrote that she was rich, accomplished, and good. With all that it would be too much to demand that a young lady should be attractive, as well. Does she like Paris, or would she prefer to reside in America?"

"In America, of course," replied Barbara.

"That is good, I have myself often thought of visiting New York. I am in a business which they tell me would be very lucrative over there. We manufacture wines."

"I do not think that grapes are cultivated sufficiently in America, to make that a very profitable business there."

"But we do not make genuine wines. We simply imitate them. Our firm can furnish an exact duplicate of any required wine, with the flavor, color, and bouquet, so exactly rendered, that the most expert connoisseur would be deceived, and that without the use of a single grape."

"What do you use then?"

"Brandy, dye-wood, vitriol, and powerful essences."

"But the result must be poisonous."

"Most certainly, but there is a great deal of money in it."

"I think that is simply horrible."

"You object to the business. On what grounds?"

"It would be illegal in our country. It must result in ruin every way, to the bodies and souls of your customers."

Monsieur Armand looked at her in wide-eyed surprise. He had never regarded his business in that light before. "Do you think," he asked meditatively, "that Mademoiselle Maud would entertain the same sentiments? Is that the reason that her sister has not come to any definite understanding with my mother? She wrote that there was some objection, and that was why I was interested to come on

CHATEAU DE FONTAINEBLEAU (THE OVAL COURT).

and see the young lady, but I thought that perhaps it was because she did not care to live in France."

They were standing in the Oval Court, surrounding which, the most interesting parts of the palace looked down upon them. The others had gone inside, and for a few moments they were alone.

"If you wish to know how Maud would feel in the matter," Barbara said slowly, "I am sure if you were to offer her this entire palace, she would refuse it if it were purchased with money obtained in such a way. But then Maud does not want to marry any one, under any circumstances."

"Mademoiselle Maud does not wish to marry," the young man replied, in some surprise, " and why is that?"

"She is too young, and she has not yet finished her course at Vassar."

"What then is this Vassar? Is it a convent, a religious house?"

"Oh, dear no, that is, it is quite religious enough, but not in the way you mean. It is a college, where we take all the higher studies, mathematical astronomy, Greek, and Latin."

"And is Mademoiselle Maud passionately devoted to Latin?"

"She detests it, but it's in the curriculum, you know, and we have to take it. She is devoted to art, and after she graduates, she intends to become an artist. She will never marry, nobody could induce her."

"But suppose I also became a great artist, could I not in that way win her admiration?"

Barbara shook her head. "She would not care for you unless you turned out a genius, and you do not look in the least like one."

CHAPTER III.

JOAN OF ARC'S TOWN.

AWAY from fascinating Paris, with its parks and palaces, its gaiety and pathos, our travellers whirled into the heart of the sunny south of France. They paused at historic picturesque Chartres only long enough to make an excursion to the Chateau de Maintenon, the home of the lovable and witty little woman whose misfortune it was to attract the attention of Louis XIV., and to be raised to the onerous dignity of court life. Her letters tell what a slavery it was. "Dear me," exclaimed Saint, as they stood beside the moat and viewed the beautiful old castle with peaked and turreted roofs, its girouettes and balconies, "not even this lovely palace and the honor of being a king's wife could compensate me for the society life she led, the being preyed upon by every member of the court, having to settle their quarrels and intrigues, to hear and sympathize with all their grievances and ambitions, and in living completely for others, have no life left for herself."

"She called herself a mushroom," said Maud, "I can imagine that a mushroom might have been pretty well torn and crushed between such thistles and rocks of grandees."

From Chartres the quartette passed at once to Orleans, the city so closely identified with the history of its renowned Maid. They found her statue in front of the city hall, and an interesting old museum devoted almost exclusively to souvenirs of her career. But what interested the girls most was the succession of captivating old houses, still standing, from whose mullioned windows and quaintly carved balconies high-bred dames had witnessed the enthusiastic

CHATEAU DE MAINTENON.

demonstrations of the people who thronged about the deliverer of their city. Everything here reminded the spectator of the victorious part of the career of Joan of Arc, of her knightly exploits and beatific visions and of the unanimous gratitude and worship of the rescued

VIEW OF CHARTRES.

people of France. When she trod this soil she was adored almost as a supernatural person, there was nothing to suggest the mock examination in prison, torture and the death of the stake. They found that they could secure lodgings for a few days in one of these historic houses, a fascinating old mansion with a noble spiral staircase of white stone, and a great carved chimney-piece, fit for a baronial hall. A pillared colonnade partly surrounded the central court, and grotesque gargoyles craned their necks from under the eaves. The place had fallen from its ancient state, and was occupied now by a cooper, whose kegs and cheese-boxes were piled in the grand salon until they touched the armorial ornaments of the ceiling. It seemed like going back to the middle ages to find themselves actually established in a building dignified by the name of Agnes Sorel's house, and Saint was sure that one night she heard the clank of armor as though the knightly Dunois were keeping guard in the court below. This clanking proved afterward to be the creaking of the windlass with which the family drew water from the cistern.

"What a lovely old place it is!" said Maud. "It is like moving about in one of Scott's romances. I would rather a thousand times live in a house like this than to have my choice of all the princely modern buildings in America."

"It would not take much of a fortune to buy it," suggested Mrs. Arnold, "and Madame Le Prince told me she was not at all mercenary in regard to her son. She only requires as dowry for his wife as much money as they will give him. Now this old place might be bought for a song, and Papa Le Prince with all his antiquarian taste would be just the person to restore and furnish it."

"Lily," exclaimed Maud with some indignation, "I do not desire to hear that young man mentioned again. I trust we have done with him forever."

"I must say, Maud," expostulated Mrs. Arnold, in an aggrieved manner, "from the way in which you take me to task, one would imagine that I was travelling under your care, instead of having been constituted your adviser in points of social etiquette."

Maud bit her lips, " Well, Lily, I trust this is our last disagreement. We are off now for fresh fields and pastures new, and you don't know

JOAN IN PRISON.

how thankful I am that you have no acquaintances in the south of France, and that, consequently, there will be no social etiquette to be observed."

"I don't know about that," mused Mrs. Arnold, "one sometimes runs across old friends where they are least expected, and then it is one of the privileges of travel, that you are constantly making new and valuable acquaintances."

"One can make acquaintances at home," Barbara suggested, "and it seems a pity to waste our time while abroad, in cultivating people, when there are so many more interesting things to be done. I propose that we make Orleans our headquarters, and make excursions all around the country, to the historic chateaux of France."

"Orleans is really quite a central point," assented Saint; "we can radiate around it until we have exhausted the chateaux in its immediate vicinity, and then move our tents a stage southward."

Barbara took out her guide-book. "Let us go first to Bourges; it is not far, and there is an exceedingly interesting old castle, the 'Chateau du Moutier,' in the neighborhood."

To Bourges accordingly an excursion was planned for the next day, but when the morning arrived, Mrs. Arnold awoke with a severe headache. Their tickets had been purchased, and it seemed a pity to forfeit them.

"You will be all right to-morrow, Lily," said Maud; "why not let us go on and secure rooms for you? We can meet you at the station when you arrive."

Mrs. Arnold demurred. She was afraid to trust them alone, and imagined all sorts of dangers which girls might run without the protection of a married lady. She yielded the point rather unwillingly, stipulating only that Fifine, the daughter of the cooper, should accompany them in a bonne's cap and apron, as a hostage to respectability. It was in vain that Maud protested that they were not babies, and did not need a nurse tagging about with them. Mrs.

Arnold was inexorable, and Fifine, with round, smiling face, and great wondering eyes, took her first ride in a rail-car as guardian of Maud's sketch-box, Saint's waterproof, and a lunch-basket prudently provided by Barbara.

They arrived safely at Bourges, secured their room, and visited the interesting Hotel de Ville, once the home of doughty Jacques Coeur, then engaged a barouche and driver to take them to the Chateau du Moutier, on the morrow, and retired early, with high anticipations of a day of pleasure. The next day the girls hurried to the station, but to their astonishment the train whizzed by, leaving no Mrs. Arnold.

FIFINE AS BONNE.

"Lily is always behind hand," said Maud. "I might have known that she would get left if I were not there to hurry her up."

But the next train from the north disappointed them again.

"Perhaps her illness was more serious than we imagined," suggested Saint.

"I will go back at once," exclaimed Maud, impulsively.

"Better telegraph first," advised Barbara. They waited anxiously two or three hours. The telegram received no reply.

"There is a train north at four this afternoon, and I shall return by it to Orleans," said Maud, who was almost distracted.

"We will go with you," exclaimed the other girls. They returned to the hotel, lunched, paid their bills, collected their belongings, and found themselves at the station just as the train from the south rolled in. Maud rushed to one of the doors, but was deterred from entering by a lady who was alighting, — it was Mrs. Arnold.

"Lily, Lily!" she exclaimed. "How ever did you manage to get on this train? Were you carried by, this morning?"

"Yes, Maud, dear," replied Mrs. Arnold faintly. "I have been quite ill. I had a queer sort of fit in the railway carriage, and completely lost consciousness for a time."

"My poor Lily," cried Maud penitently, "I ought not to have left you."

"You know I did not approve of it," replied Mrs. Arnold, with a superior air; "I think that this proves that we should always travel together. I do not know what would have become of me if I had not happened to have made the acquaintance of an English lady who occupied the same compartment with myself. I will tell you all about it when we reach the hotel, but really I am too faint now to speak."

After dinner the whole story came out. "We were alone in the compartment," explained Mrs. Arnold, "and you don't know how thankful I was to have so pleasant a travelling companion. When she said that she was English, I asked her if she knew the Baroness Burdett-Coutts, and she said that she was her first cousin by marriage; then of course I felt perfectly free to converse with a person so highly connected. She said that she had sent her cousin on in advance to secure rooms for her, and she was very glad of my company, for she had valuable jewels about her, and one meets so many unprincipled characters while travelling. You would have been very much interested in her conversation. She knew the legend connected with every old ruin on the way, for she had been over the route a number of times. I wonder if you noticed a barren stretch of country on the way, a sort of heath without a vestige of a tree or shrub. She said it had originally been one of the most fertile spots in France, but a company set up some chemical works and the fumes poisoned the vegetation for miles around. 'If you open the window,' she said, 'you can perceive the chemicals quite plainly.' And so I did, a faint, sickening odor, which made me feel quite ill. 'Oh!' I said, 'it is suffocating;' and I put down the sash. 'Yes,' she replied; 'you look quite faint, — take my vinaigrette.' I took a good sniff at it, but it was too late. I felt myself going, going, and was only conscious that my friend drew me gently to her, and fanned me with her handkerchief. When I came to myself the train was stopping at Nevers, and I was quite alone."

THE BARONESS'S COUSIN.

"It is very extraordinary," mused Barbara, "I should have thought your friend would not have deserted you until you recovered."

"The worst of it was," continued Mrs. Arnold, "that when I came to buy my return ticket to Bourges, I found that I had been robbed, my purse was gone, my watch and chain, and the gold inlaid opera glass that I bought in Paris as a wedding present for Blanche Bellmont, — I thought that there would be no harm in my using it on this trip, as I left mine at Fontainebleau. Well, they were all gone, and if I hadn't happened to have put some change in the pocket of my reticule I am sure I don't know how I should ever have got back to you. I can't conceive how the thief got all the things without my knowledge. He must have been more adroit than our New York pickpockets."

"Lily, you are a baby!" exclaimed Maud. "Can you not see that it was your travelling companion who robbed you?"

CHATEAU DU MOUTIER.

"Maud Van Vechten, can you imagine that a relative of the Baroness Burdett-Coutts would do such a thing?"

"Of course not, but what makes you so sure that she is a relative of the Baroness? You have only her word for it."

"Do you think she took advantage of my happening to faint?"

"There was n't a single happen about it," asserted Barbara, confidently, "all that story about the chemical works was a clever fabrication,—the creature chloroformed you!"

"I am afraid you are right, and I wonder I did not suspect her at the time." Mrs. Arnold was extremely mortified by the occurrence, and for a time her self-confidence was considerably shaken.

The next morning the party visited the Chateau du Moutier, a massive-walled deep-dungeoned castle, more like a feudal fortress than any edifice which they had yet seen. At its foot flowed the peaceful river Cher, and the prince of the power of the air shrieked about its battlements, rattled its rusty weather-cocks until their creaking resembled the cries and wailing of prisoners undergoing torture, and buffeted the tattered gonfalons that flaunted defiance from the topmost pinnacles. After this excursion they returned to Orleans for a few days, which Maud improved in sketching, and Saint and Barbara by prowling in the Museum. Barbara was often seen during these days with note-book and pencil. "Are you preparing a history of Joan of Arc?" Maud asked jestingly, "if so, I hope you will engage me to illustrate it."

"You need not laugh," Barbara replied, I am going to have all my compositions for next year written up before we return."

"You must read us your essay on Joan of Arc when it is finished."

"With pleasure," Barbara replied, but the essay was never finished, for the next day the party continued its journey to Blois.

CHAPTER IV.

AN HISTORIC CHATEAU.

AT Blois, of course the first object of interest was the royal chateau, — a building fated to be the theatre of many tragedies. It seemed to the girls that the very spirit of crime lurked still in the

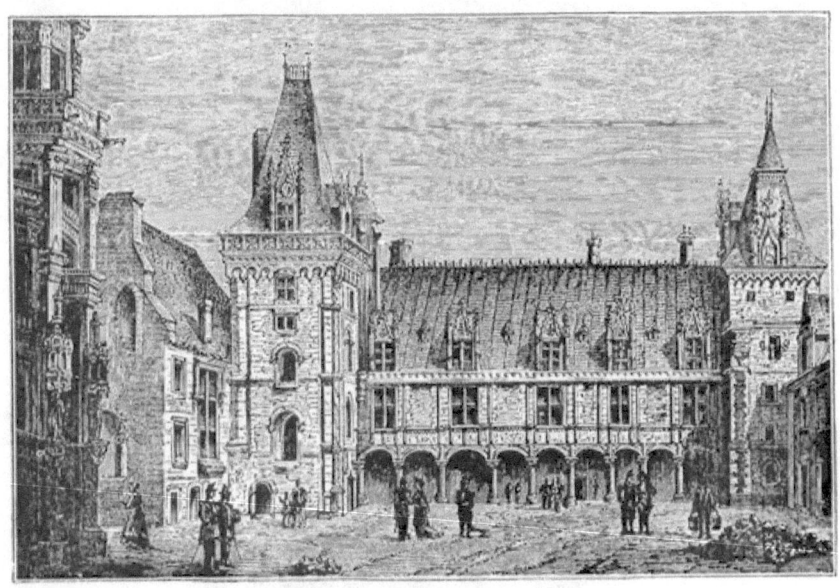

CHATEAU DE BLOIS, EAST SIDE.

guilt-haunted corridors. The gargoyles looked at one another with malicious, knowing glances, as who should say, — "We know and we

CHATEAU DE BLOIS, FROM THE NORTH.

could tell such secrets of treason, treachery, and murder. We have overheard conspiracies, and acted as spies upon scenes of infamy and atrocity. We understood the intrigues of Catherine de Medicis, stony-hearted and unpitying as ourselves. The great Duc de Guise looked up at us and shuddered as he saw something sinister in our expressions when he strode into the chateau to his death. We have not only known all this, but we have instigated it, for we are fossil demons, spirits of evil, who brooded over these battlements to tempt their occupants to guilt, and who have been turned to stone, in expiation of our crimes."

The girls found a great part of the chateau preserved in its original state, and were shown the blood-stains on the floor of the room where Guise fell at the foot of the royal bed, pierced by the assassin's daggers. The weak king, Henri III., came, and looked at his fallen enemy and quailed before him. "How tall he is!" he cried, "he looks even taller than when he was alive."

> "There was a manhood in his look,
> Which murder could not kill."

After the royal chateau, they visited a smaller one, originally the residence of the Duc de Guise, but which had been purchased in these latter days, and conscientiously restored by a noted historical painter, Leon Escosura. Monsieur Escosura was absent at his Parisian studio, where Maud had met him; but he had courteously given her a card to his housekeeper, who now showed the party the little jewel-box of a chateau, gossipping garrulously about the rooms and objects which she showed them. The girls were somewhat familiar with the paintings of Escosura, having seen them at Goupil's gallery in New York, and it was extremely interesting to them to visit his atelier, especially as at Blois he kept his wonderful wardrobe, a museum of antique stuffs probably unsurpassed by any private, and by few public collections. Here were faded Arras and Gobelin tapestries, tufted Aubusson carpets, silken and satin hangings dropping to pieces with their own weight. Here were ecclesiastical vestments of marvellous embroidery, and altar-cloths of old rose-point. Here were costumes too, of the very period of Catherine de Medicis, and which were very probably worn by ladies of her court; royal velvets whose sumptuous masses of light and shade were rimed with a delicate bloom like a dust of white ashes over a living coal, an effect which only age can give, and which artists love to render, and satin with a flickering sheen evanescent as mother-of-pearl, and exquisite in flow and fold, as in tint. Maud did not wonder that Escosura had seemed to her, across the water, as rather a painter of costume than a figure painter, that his gold-wrought brocades seemed fairly to rustle in his pictures, their flowered patterns passing from light to shadow with admirable skill, while his faces were often lacking in character and expression.

"It is not the highest art, after all," she said, as the gate of the chateau clanged behind them. "How much more glorious it is to be a painter of feeling, like Millet, and paint the souls of men and women looking out of patient, pleasant faces, instead of all this trumpery of theatrical costume."

"That is true," replied Saint; "but every artist is not a genius like Millet, and these historical pictures and old costumes do bring up the past very vividly, and with a bon-bon box in my hand that once held poisoned confections, and was itself held by the wicked fingers of the king mother and murderess, I can believe that she really lived, and that history is not mere romance."

"How much more we enjoy these things," suggested Barbara, "from seeing them after we have completed the course in history. I am so glad we happened to be in advance of our class, in that department. I can well imagine that to one who knew nothing of the

MURDER OF THE DUC DE GUISE.

events at the time when the chateau of Blois was in its prime, a visit to this old town would be a bore."

"It seems to me," assented Saint, "that a visit to Europe before one had studied history would be a great mistake."

"I never studied history to any great extent," placidly remarked Mrs. Arnold; "and yet I enjoy coming to Europe."

"I am sure you have not smiled once since we came to Blois," Maud declared.

"By your own make out, history would hardly have made the place gayer for me," retorted Mrs. Arnold; "besides, I expected to receive a letter from Madame Le Prince, which has not arrived. I shall doubtless find it waiting for me at Madrid."

Maud scowled. "I thought we had seen the last of Madame Le Prince," she murmured.

"Maud, dear," exclaimed Barbara; "I think studios are fascinating places, especially when one has the means to purchase a chateau and fit it up like Monsieur Escosura. I bespeak a chance to accompany you on any further visits of the kind. Do you remember Belle Branscomb's experience when she went to see Kaulbach's studio in Germany? She knocked at the door, and a little old man opened it, and listened to her request to see Herr Kaulbach, while he nibbled away at a bit of cheese.

"'The artist Kaulbach is at his luncheon,' he said, 'but I will show you his paintings.' He then took them to the studio, and was politely attentive, and as he seemed to take an interest in his master's work, Belle was quite free with him, and made very frank remarks and criticisms upon the pictures, which seemed to amuse the old man greatly, especially when anything she said was unfavorable. It gradually dawned upon Belle that this man, whom she had mistaken for the janitor, was no other than Kaulbach himself."

"Was he really?"

"Of course he was, and he had told the truth when he said that Kaulbach was at lunch, for he kept eating his bread and cheese while showing them the studio."

"Tours is the next stopping-place," said Maud; "but I believe hardly a vestige remains of the chateau of Plessis lez Tours, which Walter Scott immortalized in his romance of Quentin Durward."

"It seems a pity, with all our western wealth, we do not build chateaux in America," said Saint.

"We do better," replied Barbara. "We build colleges. And indeed, Vassar resembles a French chateau more than I would have thought. Just wait till the vines have a chance to grow, and the dear old pile to mellow into venerable age; and Vassar, in the midst of her noble park, will be able to hold up her head, for picturesque interest, with any ducal chateau in sunny France."

"But Vassar has no noble sculptures or glorious stained glass," sighed Maud.

"She will have," Barbara replied, impetuously. "Girls don't usually have a great many jewels. Vassar is young yet, she will gain her diamonds as years go by. She has done enough for us, and it is for us girls to decorate her in return. I am sure the stained glass of La Farge and Tiffany rivals the medieval windows we see over here. When I come into my property I mean to make the chapel a present of one memorial window, and that will make the others look so mean, that other alumnæ may be will be minded to complete the set."

"I intend to study painting on glass," said Maud. "Perhaps some day I can create something worthy to be placed there."

"I have neither the money to purchase nor the skill to make a window," said Saint. "What can I do for Vassar?"

"Be a window!" exclaimed Barbara, quoting from her favorite poet, George Herbert, —

"Man is a brittle and a crazy glass,
 Yet in Thy temple thou dost him afford,
 This glorious and transcendent place,
 To be a window, through Thy grace.
 Making Thy life to shine within,
 Which else shows wat'rish, bleak, and thin."

A WINDOW.

CHAPTER V.

OCEAN AND MOUNTAINS.

"THE strength of the hills is His also. The sea is His, and He made it," chanted the choir of the tiny English chapel at St. Jean de Luz, a little town just on the frontier of Spain. At the right the Atlantic rolled gloriously in to the throat of the Bay of Biscay, and toward the left the grand chain of the Pyrenees stepped majestically down to the sea.

After leaving Tours the party had paused only for a night at Bordeaux, and then had come a stretch of desolate, sandy country, known as the Landes, where peasants upon stilts tended their flocks, and were sometimes to be seen, propped by a long pole, knitting composedly, while their charges browsed upon the scanty herbage. They found St. Jean de Luz to be a favorite watering-place of the English. A few families, who came only to enjoy the sea-bathing for a few weeks, had been unable to resist the fascination of the place, and, remaining, formed a small English colony, with chapel, and rector, and circulating library of English books. Fashionable Biarritz, near by, was a favorite sea-side resort of the French. There were immense hotels and the Empress's villa, and there was all the rabble of the Parisian *monde*, with fireworks and brass bands *ad libitum*. But here at St. John of the Light there was a crumbling old town, encroached upon by the relentless sea, so that at low-tide one could see the foundations of houses draped with algae, and serving as aquaria for nations of fishes. Here were sturdy Basque fishermen and bold, black-eyed girls in *alpa gatas*, or curious white canvas sandals laced around their shapely ankles with vivid scarlet braid.

Votive offerings of tiny ships suspended before the altars of the churches in this region told of what were considered miraculous escapes on the stormiest of waters

"In the Bay of Biscay, O."

Across the bay shimmered the domes and roofs of the old Spanish

A LEAF FROM MAUD'S SKETCH-BOOK.

town of Fontarabia; further down the coast was San Sebastian, where bull-fights were sometimes celebrated. The mountain of Trois Couronnes showed its triple peak in the background, now purple with cloud shadows, now rosy with reflected sunset light. Little donkeys, gaily caparisoned with a multitude of scarlet tassels and jingling bells, were ready to take them in any direction by land, and the fishing boats were always tempting them seaward. One night the Bay showed them what it could do in the shape of a storm. The surges pounded the beach like trip-hammers, the wind howled demoniacally, and shook the hotel, which faced the sea, until the light iron bedsteads in which they lay seemed fairly to be lifted from the shore. In the morning they saw that a large English steamer, homeward bound from the Mediterranean, had put in behind the breakwater, as the sea was too heavy outside for her to proceed on her course.

"What atrocious weather!" said Mrs. Arnold, as they sat at breakfast. "I never could endure lightning, and the thunder reminded me of a Fourth of July celebration at home."

"I thought it simply glorious," exclaimed Saint. "It made me think of the 'Hail mingled with fire' in the Israel in Egypt. It was the grandest music I have heard since we came abroad."

The beach was strewn with masses of sea-weed torn up by the storm, lying tangled like cordage of stranded ships. The storm was, however, an exceptional occurrence. The weather during the greater part of their stay was fine, and the long stretch of yellow sand was gay with bathers frolicking on the beach or floundering like playful porpoises in the breakers.

Maud carried her camp-stool to a sheltered nook, and filled her sketch-book with amusing groups, making a pretty picture herself, with her earnest face and unconscious attitude. They lingered as long as they could in the restful old place, and then turned their faces toward the mountains.

"Nothing in France," says an English writer, "is more beautiful than the Basque Pyrenees." The magnificent scenery of the higher ranges is hardly surpassed by Switzerland itself. St. Sauveur, the Pic du Midi, Luchon, Cauterets and Les Eaux Chauds are each romantically or wildly picturesque. Besides the natural attractions there are fascinating historical remains; old Templar churches at St. Savin and Luz, and an interesting citadel at St. Jean Pied de Port, guarding the entrance into Spain. Through a portion of the Pyrenees, therefore, the girls resolved to go. They set out from Bayonne on the top of a shambling old diligence for St. John of the Citadel, and bowled through most interesting mountain scenery, now slowly climbing the steep ramps, and now dashing recklessly downward at headlong speed. They passed the Pas de Roland, which the peasants say he hacked through the mountain with his wonderful sword Durandal, a sword said to have been preserved with the hero's topboots for centuries at the Convent of Roncesvalles. After a long day's ride they found themselves in queer old St. Jean de Port, under the shadow of Vauban's mighty fortress. The Convent of Roncesvalles was only a day's journey across the mountains, and the girls decided to

MAKING A PICTURE HERSELF.

make it on mule-back, hiring a sturdy mountaineer as guide, who trudged contentedly at their side, encouraging the animals with astounding whacks. They sat on strange pack-saddles, and it being a matter of no consequence as to which side they faced, they placed themselves in opposite positions, in order to catch the scenery on both sides of the road.

The convent is celebrated as built beside the long and narrow defile where Roland and his men were surprised and massacred.

Charlemagne was returning, as the history goes, from a victorious campaign against the Moors in Spain. Roland, his kinsman, prefect of the marches of Brittany, commanded the rear of his army. Entangled in the ravine, the mountaineers fell upon them, hurling down

ON MULEBACK.

great stones and trunks of trees, and massacred to a man. Roland died waking the echoes with his wild horn. Its appeal for help, so says tradition, was heard by Charlemagne ninety miles away, who hurried back with his army, but all too late. When the Pyrenean mountaineers hear the wind uttering strange and demoniacal wailings

DEATH OF ROLAND.

through the gorges of the mountains, they say still, "It is the re-echoing of Roland's death cry."

The song of Roland is the oldest Christian ballad extant. It tells the story as Tasso might have done. The passage which tells of Charlemagne's arrival upon the field is especially good, —

> "How high the mountains and the beetling crags!
> How deep the gorges, and how swift the streams
> Loud blow the trumpets of the Emperor;
> Before, behind, the army loud they blow,
> And answer Roland's horn.
>
> The Emperor rides on in bitter wrath,
> The French are furious with agony.
> Not one who is not sobbing as he rides;
> Not one who is not praying God to save
> Roland in mercy till they reach the field,
> And deal brave blows beside him. All in vain;
> It is too late. Alas! they come too late!"

The convent library was filled with ancient books and many relics which reminded the beholder of the age of Charlemagne. "That must have been an interesting school," said Saint, "which he established in his palace, presiding over it himself, and giving out to his sages questions and problems in logic, astronomy, geometry, and even theology."

The men whom they met upon the road had the look of brigands. They carried heavily loaded sticks called *makillahs*, and wore sanguinary colored turbans, or *boinas*. "They look," said Barbara, "as if they might belong to the clan that murdered Roland."

"They were all Carlists at heart," their guide said, "and have, most of them fought for the pretender, in the late wars. They live now by smuggling the fiery wines of Spain into France."

Even the girls were wild as the goats they tended. They wore, as did the men, dark cloth jackets gayly trimmed with braid, the only difference being that their own were generally sleeveless, displaying their dimpled elbows and the wide, white chemise sleeves. "I wonder whether they are called Basques from this peculiarity in their costume," queried Mrs. Arnold. "More likely that we have adopted

PEPITA.

the jacket and the name Basque from them," replied Maud. They were coquettish in their unconscious poses, and there was one gypsy-like creature, who occupied a room into which they could look from

CHARLEMAGNE'S SCHOOL OF THE PALACE.

their hotel balcony, who seemed to have a craving after civilization, for she had a wee bit of a cracked glass, before which she was continually combing her stiff, black hair. But an evil-looking gun with a bent bayonet, hung above the glass. It belonged to Pepita's father, and had seen service; moreover, it was ready to be handled again, and some one told them of a fierce song which Basque Carlists were wont to sing as they dashed to their terrible hand-to-hand encounters, —

> "They are not worth our powder,
> So thrift should be shown,
> The bayonet, the bayonet!
> The bayonet alone."

Once more upon the rail, the girls left the Pyrenees behind them, with all their fascination and terror, their savage gorges, and picturesque peasants, crumbling architecture, and wild legends. Over dizzy trestle-work, and through cavernous tunnels, out into blinding sunshine, past riotous cascades, sleepy villages, dusty olive-groves, and long stretches of tawny sun-burnt lands, they whirled into a land of romance and mystery, into the heart of Spain.

CHAPTER VI.

MADRID.

THE girls were leaning upon the wrought iron balcony, and looking out upon the fountain, whose crystal columns flashed and shattered in the basin which formed the centre of the Puerta del Sol, when Mrs. Arnold joined them with a face radiant with satisfaction.

"I knew you would like Madrid," said Maud, before her sister had time to speak, "it bears such a close resemblance to your beloved Paris."

"It is not that alone," replied Mrs. Arnold, "though I do confess that the sights of a city are more to my taste than those tiresome chateaux and the barbaric places we found in the Pyrenees, but I have just received a letter from Madame Le Prince."

"Did she return your opera glass?" Maud asked, dryly.

"No, but her son will return it for her in person."

Maud turned with a start, "We are not likely to meet that youth again, I hope."

"Indeed we are; he is at this moment somewhere in Spain, probably Valencia."

"So glad we are not going to Valencia."

"But he will find us out, never fear. He has changed his business; he has become an artist, and Madame Le Prince hints that it is all out of love for you."

Maud flushed indignantly. "One does not become an artist all of a sudden. He will not succeed in that or in anything else."

"Wait till you see. Madame Le Prince says his 'creations' have been much praised, and that the best critics have lauded his exquisite taste, especially in dainty harmonies of tint."

"It would be remarkable, would it not?" exclaimed Barbara, "if that young man should turn out an artist. Even if he only makes a poor one, it is certainly a more innocent occupation than an agent for counterfeit wines."

"He will only be a counterfeiter in any case, I fear," replied Maud, scornfully.

"Really, Maud, you are too bad," exclaimed Barbara, hotly. "I never saw any one arrange a bouquet so charmingly as he did. He had the true artist's eye for color and a poet's feeling for sentiment. I take that young man under my special protection, and you are not to speak of him in a *desultory* manner."

The girls laughed merrily. "At your old tricks, Barb," Saint remarked mildly, for Barbara had been noted in her preparatory days at College, for a reckless use of long words when enthusiastic or excited.

"Which do you mean, derogatory or insulting?"

"Both, of course. I had time to get only one out and I wanted to make it strong."

Mrs. Arnold saw that nothing was to be gained by pursuing the subject, and gracefully eluded further discussion of this point, by suggesting another—

"What do you think, girls, of attending a bull-fight?"

"A bull-fight? horrible!"

"Lily, are you crazy?"

"Vassar girls at a bull-fight, the *idea!*"

"Why not? The spectacle is the national amusement of Spain, you lose one of your opportunities."

"I don't care," exclaimed Maud, "they are low and vulgar, and brutal, I would as soon think of attending a prize-fight in London, or a cock or dog-fight,"—

"Or a hanging in Kansas," added Barbara, "or even a New York walking-match. Why we are all of us members of the Society for Prevention of Cruelty to Animals. I think I see myself trotting coolly off to a bull-fight — on Sunday morning too!"

STUDYING VELASQUEZ.

Mrs. Arnold laughed at the tempest which she had raised. "Well, *this* is not Sunday," she remarked, "what do you suggest for to-day?"

"The Royal Art Gallery, of course," replied Maud, "it is the sight of sights in Madrid. Nowhere else can you see Velasquez to advantage, for nearly all his works are owned here."

Maud carried her sketch-box, and Barbara accompanied her to wander through the seemingly endless galleries with her guide-book, her eyes dilating with awe and admiration before the superb Titians, chief among which she admired his portrait of himself, painted in his old age, and the Charles V. on horseback. There were dashing equestrian figures by Velasquez, — his Tapestry Weavers, the Forge of Vulcan, the Surrender of Breda, Philip IV.'s Family and Dwarfs, and other master-pieces which chained her attention as well, while Maud laughingly charged her with being lost "in wonder, love and praise," as she stood before Murillo's Immaculate Conception.

Here were treasures, too, by the old Flemish masters which were secured during the reign of Philip IV., when Spain ruled the Netherlands. Barbara, who was familiar with Motley's great history, was not surprised to find here gems by Rubens, Vandyke, and the lesser Dutch painters. The horrible pictures of Ribera were chronicles of the Inquisition, the dark days of torture and the *auto da fé*.

Saint came across a strange old man, who seemed peculiarly out of place in the Spanish capital. He was an Englishman, George White by name, though he presented a dirty enamelled card bearing the Spanish version of his name, Jorge Blanco. He had come into Spain twenty years previous as tutor for a young hidalgo, and had picked up a precarious existence, principally as guide and courier for English tourists ever since. He had always intended to return to England, but had never been able to lay by sufficient money for his travelling expenses. Saint pitied the poor old man, he seemed to her like an old wreck stranded upon a strange shore, and she engaged his services as guide while they remained in Madrid. The girls found the city more interesting the longer they remained in it.

Its open-air theatres and gardens, where strange ices with stranger names were served in tall glasses, while bands played, fireworks glittered, and fountains plashed; its ever varying street panoramas; their shopping expeditions after lace, *almagro* mantillas, and Spanish blond scarfs; the luxury of the royal palace, and the lesson in history afforded by the state carriages of different epochs displayed at the royal palace, all blended afterward in a dazzling mental kaleidoscope of shifting scenes and figures.

They made an excursion to the Escorial, a huge, whity-gray, prison-like building, which has looked down forbiddingly upon Madrid from a windy mountain spur for three centuries. A great convent, palace, museum, barracks, college, tomb, the wearied eyes and feet of the girls soon pronounced it a stupendous bore. The exterior was extremely bald, not a spray of ivy or moss to give to the bleak iron stone the dignity of age; it had the bare, forbidding look of a penitentiary. Within, it consisted of a labyrinth of cloisters, halls, court-yards, cells and corridors connecting the pantheon, library, palace, refectory, sacristy, etc.

The Escorial was built by the bigot king, Philip II., who lived here for fourteen years, half a monk, and died miserably in a little cell behind the high altar, where he could view through a little window the elevation of the Host. The library was a most tempting hall. On lecterns were displayed Hebrew Bibles, copies of the Koran in Arabic, and some Latin books. Maud was desirous of copying some Moorish illuminations. She knew that the Inquisitor Cisneres had burned 80,000 Arabic volumes taken from the Caliph Abdurahaman's immense library at Cordova, but that some, thanks to the beauty of their decoration, had been saved from the flames and safely stowed away in the Escorial. The books on the library shelves, apparently never having been intended to be read, had all been carefully turned with their edges outward. Maud requested Jorge Blanco to beseech the priest in charge to place the coveted volumes at her disposal. The two conversed some time with much vigor, and at length the guide explained to Saint, whom he persisted in regarding as the chaperone of the party, that the priest was much shocked by her proposal, and that such a privilege was not to be thought of without a special dispensation from his sanctity the high-cardinal-patriarch arch something or other. If the senoras could remain in the vicinity for several weeks *they might take measures to institute inquiries as to the advisability of requesting the Superior of the institution to forward her written request to this high functionary, who had now departed on a pilgrimage to Rome or Jerusalem.*

"It seems very strange to me," said Saint, a few days afterward, "that the capital city of Spain has no cathedral."

"Toledo is so near and handy by," suggested Barbara.

"And the Escorial answers the purpose very well," added Maud.

"I have just had such an interesting visit at the Convent of

THE LIBRARY OF THE ESCORIAL.

Atocha," continued Saint, "I must take you girls out there before we leave Madrid. They have an image of the Virgin there, one of whose perquisites it is to possess the wedding dresses of all the Queens of Spain. Barbara would just revel in the collection."

THE COURIER EXPLAIN

And here we interrupt our narrative to describe one of the curious features of religious worship in Spain — a feature which they met continually as they became more familiar with the cathedrals and churches of the country, and which exists here in a phase different from that of any other Catholic country.

CHAPTER VII.

THE DEVOTIONAL IMAGES OF SPAIN.

ENTERING Spain from the north, and visiting in order its fascinating old cities, from Barcelona to Malaga, we find that our itinerary includes a series of grandiose cathedrals rich in interest to the student of history, of art, or of human nature.

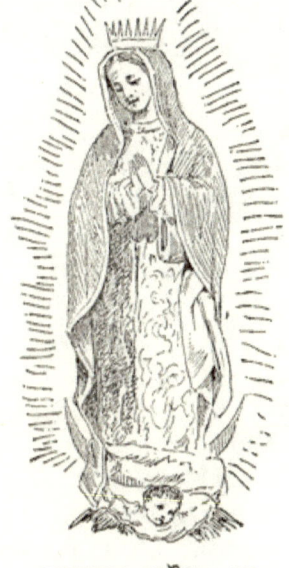

NUESTRA SEÑORA DE GUADALUPE.

In each of these cathedrals is to be found an image of the Virgin, sometimes of great age and often decorated with jewels. These images have different provinces assigned to them, and are considered as separate and distinct personages.

Nuestra Señora da Guadalupe is besought by all captives and prisoners; the royal family enjoy the special protection of the Virgin of Atocha; cripples seek the wonder-working shrine of *Nuestra Señora del Pilar;* the insane are under the care of the sacred image of Valencia; soldiers go through military evolutions before our Lady of Battles in the Cathedral of Seville; while the Virgins of Monserrat, of Toledo, and other shrines, divide the odd corners of territory not pre-empted by the sovereign ladies already mentioned.

The girls first made the acquaintance of Nuestra Señora del

Pilar in a trip which they made to the city of Zaragoza. The legend goes that the Mother of our Lord, while still living, was borne by angels to Zaragoza, and, descending upon an alabaster column, appeared to the consolation of St. James, who was then laboring in Spain. How the sacred image, which is small, and carved from black wood, appeared, and was set apart to call to mind this miraculous apparition, is not stated. The Cathedral was built for the express purpose of sheltering the sacred pillar, and a domed and profusely ornamented chapel serves as throne-room for the Virgin. The morning upon which the girls sought an audience was not set apart as a special reception day, and yet the throng of kneeling devotees was so great that they found it impossible to approach very near the august presence. As they wandered disconsolately about the outskirts of the company a beadle or other church official suggested that they might inspect the Virgin's wardrobe in the *Sagrario*. This was rare good fortune, for these trinkets are only shown on stated occasions, and all unaware they had fallen upon an exposition day. A priest reverently unlocked a spacious cabinet and showed them first the silver ware which had been presented for the Madonna's housekeeping. Here were gold and silver table services, both full size and Liliputian; silver inkstands for her use when inclined to literary pursuits; here were candlesticks without number; cups and salvers; ewers and porringers. A chest of shallow drawers ran along one side of the sacristy, resembling a case for engravings or entomological specimens. Each drawer contained a single dress, or rather fan-shaped

NUESTRA SENORA DEL PILAR.

mantle, which when fastened about the image, gave it the appearance of a large extinguisher. Each of these capes was a marvel of decorative art. There were blue velvet *manteaux* heavily embossed with embroidery in silver thread; a white satin one, stiff with arabesques in gold; strange specimens in which painting was mingled with needlework, and others a bead-work of pearls and jewels. Some of these robes had been wrought by royal ladies, and others were the patient flowering of a life spent in the cloister. There was one very peculiar, in which figures were worked in low relief, the heads consisting of miniatures painted upon ivory. The visitors were all enthusiastic, expressing their admiration by such exclamations as "*Es divino!*" Is it not Divine?

As the girls passed out of the building, jostled by repulsive beggars, their attention was attracted by the clusters of votive offerings, waxen models of legs attesting to miracles of healing performed through the intercession of the Madonna. The oil of her lamps has the reputation of restoring lost limbs, and many are the prodigies recounted. Saint remarked that the cathedral reminded her of the Pool of Bethesda in that a "multitude of impotent folk, of blind, halt and withered wait" in the porches for healing. The physicians of Spain have not a high reputation, and lamp oil, while it may not perform the wonders desired, has at least the merit of being comparatively harmless. This Virgin not only restores amputated legs, but is resorted to, to prevent broken bones. The Duchess of Abrantes hung a tiny image of our Lady del Pilar as a talisman round the neck of her favorite bull-fighter, who bore a charmed life ever after. This particular image is, perhaps, the most widely celebrated in literature. Innumerable are the legends by Catholic writers in the Spanish tongue, and her fame has crept as well into English poetry. Scott, in his description of the siege of Zaragoza, addresses the city as follows:

THE DEVOTIONAL IMAGES OF SPAIN.

> " Arise and claim
> Reverence from every heart where freedom reigns,
> For what thou worshippest! thy sainted dame,
> She of the column, honored be her name,
> By all, whate'er their creed, who honor love!"

Southey also alludes to her in the concluding stanza of Queen Mary's Christening:

> "Shine brighter now, ye stars that crown
> Our Lady del Pilar,
> And rejoice in thy grave, Cid Campeador
> Ruy Diaz de Bivar."

Between Zaragoza and Barcelona, but nearer the latter city, rise the saw-like peaks of Monserrat. Here is an ancient mountain *Hospedaria*, as interesting in its way as the Convent of St. Bernard. And here there still resides an image of the Madonna which belongs to the old *noblesse* of this peculiar aristocracy. It is supposed to have been made by St. Luke and brought to Spain by St. Peter, A. D. 50. When the Moors occupied the country it was hidden in a cave, and was discovered a century later by a bishop, who was guided to the place of concealment by a peculiarly sweet perfume, — a miracle indeed in this land of unchristian odors.

NUESTRA SEÑORA DE MONSERRAT.

Ignatius Loyola watched all night before this Virgin, dedicating himself to her as her knight, and leaving his sword on her altar before founding the order of the Jesuits. The Convent of Monserrat, like the Alpine hospices, makes a specialty of the entertainment of travellers. Ranges of wildly picturesque mountains lift their serrated outline against the sky, and warrant the name borne by the chain. The little engraving which is to be found in most religious print shops throughout Northern Spain, of this ill-favored virgin, represents as her coat of arms a range of ragged mountains crowned by a saw, the emblem of Monserrat.

Returning to Madrid, from their religious pilgrimage eastward, the girls paid their respects to the virgin of the Atocha convent, a sacred image which receives more courtly ceremonies than any other in Spain, though humbly housed in an unpretending convent. In the sacristy at the back of the altar they were shown the virgin's wardrobe, one which interested them more than that of any other image in Spain, for these dresses have each a history of their own, and were not made originally for the idol-doll to whom they now belong. The Virgin of Atocha is the patroness of the royal family, who are all married before her shrine. She has ladies of honor and dressing-maids, appointed from the ladies of the court, who robe her for state receptions and for triumphant processions. One of her perquisites is the wedding-dresses of all the queens of Spain. Our party looked over thirty of these bridal and other dresses, from Isabella the Catholic down to the wedding-robe of the present queen. Here were white satin robes with magnificent trains loaded with ermine, and blazoned in exquisite embroidery with the lion of Aragon and castles of Castile; furlongs of priceless pointe d'Espagne, citron-tinted with age, garnished with gossamer-blossom flounces, which had swept the floor of palaces, and had been carried gallantly by courtly pages. They saw the rich robe with the frightful dagger-cut in the bosom, in which Isabella II. was assassinated on her way to pay a visit to this shrine; but the only one "which angled for their eyes and caught the water," was a dainty design of Worth's, of turquoise blue satin covered with costly lace, which, in its turn, was beaded with pearls,—one of the reception dresses of the unfortunate child-queen, Mercedes.

When monarchs are so ill that their lives are despaired of, as a last resort the Virgin of Atocha is called. Basilliac writes that she paid a visit to Philip III. as he lay dying, but was powerless to arrest the approach of the darker visitant. The Virgin of Atocha, although appropriated by royalty, ranks only third in the sisterhood. El Pilar of Zaragoza stands second, but the great queen of all is, or rather was, for her prestige has waned of late, Nuestra Señora de Guadalupe. She inhabits a noble Geronomite convent, once the wealthiest in Spain, and situated in the Sierras, between Toledo and Badajoz.

The monastery, with its castellated towers, its grand library, its Gothic and Moorish cloisters, and its *hospedaria* for strangers, built with

NUESTRA SEÑORA DE LA MERCED.

NUESTRA SEÑORA DE TOLEDO.

the confiscated wealth of burnt heretics, is well worth a visit. The Virgin lost many of her personal effects during the war with the French, Napoleon's soldiers carrying away nine cartloads of solid silver from her shrine. The visitor, glancing at the canker-corroded metal work, and at the costly vestments dropping with age into silken tatters, and bearing in mind the depredations of the invader, is forcibly reminded that the Romanist has laid up his treasure "where moth and rust doth corrupt, and where thieves break through and steal." The Virgin, though no longer able to compete with her sisters in the style and magnificence suitable to so exalted a personage, bears her reduced circumstances with serene resignation. Her particular province is the liberation of captives, especially Christians held as slaves by the infidels. Her chapel is hung with broken manacles and chains, left here as votive offerings by captives rescued from the Moors. She shares this peculiar office with Nuestra Señora de la Merced, the patroness of Barcelona. A military-religious order was formed during the crusades, of knights who devoted themselves to these Virgins and to the ransom of prisoners among the Moors and Turks. Cervantes celebrated both the order and the "*Sanctissima imagen Libertad de los cautivos.*" One of the ballads which Mr. Lockhart has rescued from the mists of antiquity must have had a very vivid meaning for many a fair Spanish lady, and we can imagine that the same lips which repeated Ave Marias before Nuestra Señora de la Merced may have often sung the plaintive ballad:

NUESTRA SEÑORA D'ATOCHA.

NUESTRA SEÑORA DE LOS DESEMPARADOS.

> "Ye mariners of Spain,
> Bend stoutly on your oars,
> And bring my love again,
> For he lies among the Moors."

From Madrid the girls turned at last southward, and bidding the

THE DEVOTIONAL IMAGES OF SPAIN.

royal city a final good bye, they visited Toledo, one of the most interesting cities in all Spain. Here they found another interesting Virgin. The cathedral which shelters her is one of the noblest in the peninsula. Weeks might be spent in exploring its beauties, and a separate chapter might well be devoted to its description. The doll's crown and bracelet were stolen in 1868, but her trousseau and jewel casket as it now exists would easily furnish those of a half dozen Fifth Avenue brides. One of her mantles is embroidered with 257 ounces of pearls, 460 ounces of gold and gold thread, and eight ounces of emeralds.

NUESTRA SEÑORA DE CARMEN.

It is fabled that the Virgin descended in person to visit this image when it was first set up, and was so well pleased with it that she *kissed* it, and bestowed on it the power of working miracles. St. Ildefonso, who presided at a church upon this site at the time, was the recipient from the virgin's hands of a chasuble woven of *heavenly cloth*.

The virgin of Valencia, Nuestra Señora de los Desemparados, is the protectress of the unprotected, especially of orphans and the insane.

Nuestra Señora del Carmen, whose residence I have been unable to ascertain, is besought for souls in purgatory, and is represented in religious pictures as extending the scapulary to penitents in flames.

Wandering through the columned forest of the grand mosque of Cordova one wonders whether the religion which has usurped that of Allah in Spain has less of error in its fabric.

CHAPTER VIII.

TOLEDO.

"I NEVER heard guitar-playing before." This was Saint's exclamation, as she listened behind the curtains of her window to the chance serenade of a quartette of strolling players. The glorious moonlight transfigured the rude ramps and streets of the citadel city, the tall houses on one side were shrouded in mysterious gloom; on the other they were bathed in a flood of silver light which washed away all the unsightly stains so painfully obvious in the day, and turned the ruinous old town into a city of black marble and silver. All night they had lain awake listening to successive parties of amateurs. All Toledo seemed to be abroad serenading his ladye, and sleep was out of the question.

"I think you must have forgotten, Saint," suggested Barbara, "that we heard 'The Student of Salamanca' rendered by the Glee Club at West Point."

"No, I have not forgotten it," replied Saint, "how I wish those poor boys could hear this. Wouldn't they all cast themselves into the Hudson and drown themselves." Such an extravagant remark on the part of Saint was proof positive that she was strongly moved, for Saint was usually irresponsive, cold, and exact. She seldom made a statement which expressed either more or less than she intended, and her pet name at College had been Purity, Propriety and Precision.

By daylight Toledo showed them a city set upon a hill, with narrow precipitous streets, like defiles cut between cliffs, or cañons cut by mountain streams. These ravines were nearly all too narrow for the passage of carts or carriages; and during their entire stay in the

A STREET IN TOLEDO.

city, the girls saw only one wheeled vehicle, the diligencia, by which they arrived, and which drove directly into the interior of the hotel before stopping for them to alight. The most interesting building in Toledo, was, of course, the cathedral which has already been alluded to in the preceding chapter.

Under the domination of the Moors, Toledo was noted for its college of Magic and Alchemy. It is doubtful whether this was anything more than a school of Chemistry and Natural Science, but the reputation which it once enjoyed as supreme in the Black Art, lingers around it still. It is an oriental-appearing city. Some of these massive walls and old houses with interior courts antedate, it is very possible, the taking of the city by the Christians.

The Alcazar, an imposing building which has been used successively as palace, citadel, barrack and silk manufactory, is now utilized as a Government School. The view from its steps of the Tagus lying asleep in its bed, and the tawny plain stretching away on all sides, was extensive but not inspiring. The cathedral drew them to by it the strong magnetism of its glorious architecture, and again and again they entered its sumptuous interior. Its gilded iron work seemed to them the very gold lace of architecture.

Barbara was startled during Mass by seeing the carved figures surrounding the pulpit, which were moved by internal machinery, rise and fall upon their knees at the elevation of the Host. The cloister of this cathedral is built around the old Jews' market. The Jews helped the Christians gain Toledo from the Moors, but they must have regretted doing so afterward, for the monks circulated the falsehood that the Jews stole little children and crucified them, and so infuriated the populace that they burned the houses of the unfortunate Israelites. Frescoes in the cloister, called "The Lost Child," represent the crucifixion of a mythical boy, and serve as an apology for robbing the Jews of their market.

In a remote part of the city the girls came upon a quaint church,

INTERIOR COURT AT TOLEDO.

that of St. Juan de los Reyes. It was built by Ferdinand and Isabella, to commemorate the conquest of Granada, and the exterior walls are hung with a fringe of chains and manacles, said to have been taken from the limbs of Christian captives rescued from the land of the Moor. Isabella subsequently gave the church and convent attached, to her favorite, Cardinal Ximenes. The cloister, in the most florid style of Gothic architecture, is one of the most beautiful in Spain. A garden which resembles a hot-house gone wild, is walled in by galleries of

INTERIOR OF THE CATHEDRAL, TOLEDO.

CARDINAL XIMENES.

beautiful pointed arches and mutilated sculptures, headless saints under intricate canopies, surrounded with exuberant carved foliations, rivalled only by the blossoming oleanders, pinks, roses, and heliotrope, which clamber close to the mossy sculpture, and lay their delicate cheeks lovingly against the carved emblems. It was a place to convert one to monasticism. "Surely it would be very easy to give up the pomps and vanities of the world," said Barbara, "if one could live always in such a spot as this."

They visited the celebrated *fabrica d'armas*. Time was when a "Toledo blade" was as noted as one of Damascus, but the swords now manufactured have not the temper nor the beauty of the antique specimens displayed in the museum. Some of these had mottoes enamelled in gold upon the blade. "Do not draw me without reason, nor sheath me without honor," was a favorite, as was also the chivalric "In defence of my lady." The girls bought some daggers for the hair, of steel, beautifully encrusted with arabesque designs in gold and silver.

They left Toledo by the grand old Gate of the Sun, and looked back upon the castellated walls with regret. It was not a gay city, certainly, nor a particularly neat one, with its stable-yards invariably occupying the interior court, which was often the reception-room and dining-room as well, of the house. But it was a city with a history, and legends of enchanted palaces dating back to Roderic's time of Greek fire, fabricated for Saracen artillerymen, are still connected with its mysterious underground laboratories and windowless towers.

It remained in their memories as a type of forgotten ages, to which the time of Don Quixote, of whom they were now reminded, as they whirled through the plains of La Mancha, was modern indeed.

CHAPTER IX.

CORDOVA AND THE CALIPHATE.

THE party made their *entrée* into Cordova one evening in August. The gas-lights sparkled as they drove along the *Paseo del Gran Capitan*, so named from the famous general Gonsalvo of Cordova, one of Ferdinand's first knights in the siege of Granada. It was the principal promenade of the city, and resembled somewhat, the Prado of Madrid. During the sultry days it is deserted, and its rows of orange-trees and Japanese medlars turn their dry leaves, white with dust, to the scorching heavens. At night the scene changes. Bands play, innumerable gas-jets twinkle amongst the shrubbery, the air is delicious, and the blue dome of heaven hangs its lustrous starlamps over all. The few noble families who keep up a ghostly, antiquated state in this old town, drive up in their landaus and coaches, while the more plebeian revellers swarm the promenade, or seated at little tables, sip *horchatas de chufa* or *dulce de azahar*, a sweetmeat essentially Cordovese in character, made of orange-flowers.

In the morning Maud and Barbara started at once for the Grand Mosque, but Saint decided to spend the morning at home, for she had caught sight of an upright piano in a little reception-room that opened off the central *patio* or court of the hotel, where palms grew, a fountain plashed, and an aviary of birds made her wild to join in their music. Mrs. Arnold confessed herself a little fagged by her journey, and settled herself on a divan under an awning in the court, her dress, a whirlpool of mull ruffles, and a black-lace mantilla thrown about her head and shoulders in the Spanish fashion. Her fingers toyed with some light lace-work, but her calculating little head was full of

ANNIE LAURIE.

all manner of ambitious and romantic schemes. She had been informed by the landlord that an English party from India was stopping at the hotel. She had noted their names on the hotel register, "Lord Gubbins and suite," and she had caught a glimpse of the gentleman as she entered the breakfast-room that morning. She had not thought best to confide her plans, but she had firmly made up her mind to become acquainted with Lord Gubbins. That step once accomplished, and they should see what they should see. While these thoughts were flitting through her brain, a very distinguished looking young Englishman entered the patio, accompanied by a sour, disagreeable looking old man. Mrs. Arnold at once recognized them as Lord Gubbins and his tutor. The latter wandered restlessly about for a few moments, and then went out. The young man took up a newspaper which he glanced at listlessly but did not read. He rose at length, and Mrs. Arnold, feeling that a golden opportunity for making an acquaintance was slipping from her, looked up and asked sweetly, "If there are any English newspapers there, may I trouble you to hand me one?"

"I am sorry, madam," he replied, "these are all Spanish and French journals."

There was a pause, but the gentleman did not go, and Mrs. Arnold was racking her brains for some means of carrying on the conversation, when Saint, in the next room, all unconscious of the favor which she was conferring, turning over the leaves of her English songs and ballads, chanced to choose Annie Laurie.

The gentleman made an abrupt motion, and Mrs. Arnold, looking up, saw that there were tears in his eyes. "Pardon me, madam," he said, "the last time I heard that song was in England, five years ago."

Mrs. Arnold was charmed. "It does not seem to me," she said, "that speaking as we do, the same mother tongue, we require an introduction. I am speaking, I believe, to Lord Gubbins?"

The young man made a gesture of dissent. "My name is Featherstonhaugh. I am only Lord Gubbins' secretary."

This was indeed a disappointment, but Mr. Featherstonhaugh might prove a step toward the acquaintanceship which she desired, and Mrs. Arnold determined to cultivate him for the present. She invited him into the reception-room, introduced him to Saint, and insisted on her singing for him her entire repertoire of English songs. During the intervals of the singing, Mrs. Arnold gleaned that Mr. Featherstonhaugh was on his return from a residence in India. He was almost too impatient to reach merry England once more, to pause for a moment upon the way. But he was not the master of his own actions. Lord Gubbins preferred to leave the Mediterranean at Cartagena and to cross Spain, embarking again at Lisbon, for England; and as a member of Lord Gubbins' suite he was obliged to take the more interesting, but longer route.

For several days both parties lingered at Cordova, and the girls, though shy at first, came to feel well acquainted with Mr. Featherstonhaugh. He was a simple-mannered, brotherly sort of young man, and moreover, he was so manifestly homesick and miserable, and was so bullied and driven about by his employer, that the girls pitied him.

"That Lord Gubbins is a regular 'Old Man of the Sea,'" said Barbara, indignantly, "he orders his secretary about as though he were his lackey. In Mr. Featherstonhaugh's place I should certainly poison him."

Whenever they found him off duty the girls did their best to entertain him. His preference, they could see, was for Saint, but when Maud expressed this in confidence to Barbara, the latter exclaimed, — "Don't show that you think so for all the world. Saint would freeze into an iceberg at once."

"But Saint must know that he likes her."

"She thinks that she reminds him of a sweetheart down in Kent, but it's my opinion that he hasn't any sweetheart, or if he had one when he left England, she has probably married some one else long ere this. Dear me, just to think, here are you and Saint who are wrapped up in Art and Music, and have no heart left for anything else, and two splendid young men fall in love with you at once, — and here is little me, with no pre-occupation and never a shadow of an admirer. If this sort of thing holds out I shall go back to Colorado."

Barbara spoke lightly, in evident jest, but Maud threw her arms around her,— "You are welcome to my admirer, Barb, dear. I make over all title-deeds to that piece of property, in your favor."

"Thank you," replied Barbara, shortly, "but you undervalue Armand Le Prince when you imagine that he would give you up so lightly. I am positive that he is very much in earnest."

"Barb, you're a romantic little goose. I should never imagine that you were a Vassar girl."

"Vassar graduates do marry, sometimes; the alumnæ not infrequently bring their husbands back to exhibit them to their alma mater-in-law."

"Yes, and isn't it enough to console all the old maids, to see the line of husbands they invest in?"

Barbara shook her head. "That's because you despise all men. Now I have known two or three who were actually nice," and, — flushing a little,— "you may call me a goose if you want to, but I positively do believe I shall be married some day. I haven't the least idea to whom, and I am in no hurry about it, but I am going to make the very most of my education and of my opportunities in every way for several years to come, in order to be worthy of some good man's love."

Maud did not reply. She did not share in Barbara's feeling, but she felt that it was not a frivolous one, or a thing to be made sport of. She watched Saint with a new interest, and wondered what her views would be, though she did not quite dare to ask them.

Mr. Featherstonhaugh visited with them the great mosque, and explained the different points of Saracenic architecture, and its resemblance to that of India. He had studied architecture as a profession, and it was still his intention to become an architect; he had only gone to India with Lord Gubbins because he thought it an excellent opportunity to study the wonderful buildings of the Orient.

"While threading these dirty streets," said Saint, "we can scarcely believe that we are in the metropolis of the old Moors, the chief city of the Spanish caliphate."

"But once inside the mosque," replied Mr. Featherstonhaugh, "and does not the entire outer world become illusory and unreal? I could well believe that I hear the muezzin call, 'come to prayer, come to prayer! Prayer is better than sleep,' and the place seems peopled with shadowy forms, standing with supplicating hands, or prostrating themselves upon their prayer-rugs, their faces toward Mecca. In spite of centuries of Christian restoration and mutilation, the building has preserved its original character, and it is a mosque still."

"No cathedral has impressed me," replied Saint, "as this temple to Allah. None seems so appropriate a dwelling-place for Him who fills all space."

"That," replied the young architect, "is on account of its immense width and depth. The mind is not carried aloft as in Gothic cathedrals, by lancet windows and pointed arches. The idea of sublimity is communicated in the more difficult way, by extending dimensions laterally, and by mysterious depth. This infinitude of columns support the roof, which broods over the whole like the sense of God's beneficence, not afar but near."

"This grove of many-colored shafts is the most beautiful feature of all, to me," said Barbara. "It makes me think of the words, — 'The woods were God's first temples.'"

"The guide-book says that, originally there were twelve hundred of these columns, and over a thousand still remain."

"I did not know that stone could take so many colors," Maud remarked. "See, here are marbles from black to white, malachite green, blood-stone, black veined with chrome, ultramarine, purple porphyry, jasper, carnelian-streaked, precious lapis lazuli, and snakily mottled serpentine."

"Their history also adds an interest," continued Mr. Featherstonhaugh. "They were collected from widely distant localities; one hundred and fifteen are said to have come from Nimes and Narbonne, celebrating Moorish victories in France; sixty from the remains of Roman temples in Spain; the emperor Leo, of Constantinople, contributed one hundred and forty; while the remainder were gathered from Carthage and other African cities, from Phœnicia, Greece, Egypt, Asia Minor, and nearly every country bordering on the Mediterranean."

FATHER ST. IAGO MATAMORAS.

"It seems almost a pity, does it not," mused Barbara, "that Ferdinand and Isabella drove the Moors out of Spain? Even the religion of the country seems to have deteriorated. I am sure that Mohammedan ablutions might be introduced with good effect into the present ritual. And just look at that old priest, his face all pursed up with disgust at the little flurry of rain which will help lay this blinding dust. He does not seem to me fit to minister in the grand old mosque, and yet I've no doubt he takes as a patron, Iago *Mata-moras* (Kill the Moors) the battle saint of Spain."

"Next to the mosque," said Maud, "I think the palms that Abdurrahman planted are the most suggestive of the Moorish remains. Their feathery branches droop like funeral plumes over a a hearsed city and a buried caliphate."

CHAPTER X.

SEVILLE.

SEVILLE was a refreshing contrast to Cordova. It had a newer, cleaner, gayer look. People dressed better, and wore happier expressions. Through street doorways, curtained by a beautifully wrought iron gate,— which gave the interior the mysterious charm which a lace veil adds to a beautiful face,— the girls caught glimpses of brilliant gardens. Here were patios filled with blossoming oleanders, oriental palms and tree ferns, and the whole gamut of roses. Cacti made a battlefield of one corner, with their myriad lances and sanguinary banners, and the starry jessamine lighted a dusky recess with its elaborate lamps. In the centre, usually, a cistern or fountain, around which, ivy and passion-vine were matted, now and then they caught the white gleam of statues, the glitter of gayly enamelled faience; and sometimes a senora, fan in hand, rose tranquilly from a half hidden chair and glided away from their observation.

Again they found themselves in the same hotel with Lord Gubbins and suite, but they saw very little of Mr. Featherstonhaugh, for Lord Gubbins appeared to have noticed that he took pleasure in their society, and threw every obstacle possible in the way of their meeting.

They met him in the beautiful gardens of the Alcazar, but his employer was leaning upon his arm and whisked him away before he could scarcely more than bow. The Alcazar is a palace built for the Spanish king, Don Pedro the Cruel, by Moorish workmen under the direction of the architect of the Alhambra. The coloring and designs traced upon its walls are approached only in the finest India shawls.

Domes rise like a succession of intersecting soap-bubbles, and the stalactite stucco drops its vivid prisms in honey-comb and other intricate patterns. All this can be seen in better preservation than at the Alhambra. We feel, however, that the colors are too fresh, there is too much gilding, and after a protracted promenade through the palace, Mrs. Arnold declared that she sympathized with the Spaniards who whitewashed these walls, which their successors have since restored. The succession of brilliant, gaudy coloring fatigued their eyes, and the intricate arabesques confused and wearied their minds.

"I can imagine," said Saint, "that a king, seated in the Hall of Ambassadors, might lose the thread of a delicate bit of diplomacy while his mind was wandering in the vain attempt to trace a bit of Cufic strap-work."

The great cathedral, with the slender Giralda by its side, a tower built by the Moors, and as beautiful as the campaniles of Florence and Venice, interested them quite as much.

Seville is noted as the residence of Murillo; many of his paintings are preserved in the city. In the cathedral hangs one of surpassing beauty, a St. Francis falling into an ecstasy before the apparition of the infant Christ. Murillo seems to have had three distinctive fields of excellence. He painted equally well the Virgin and child, monks and saints moved by religious rapture, and little street-gamins, ragged brigands of the gutter. Plenty of these, with bright, saucy faces, the girls saw seated in a shadowy angle, or basking lizard-like in the sun, while they enjoyed a luncheon of a crushed melon or other luscious fruit. One little fellow, who evidently served upon occasion as altar-boy, they saw in the sacristy, divested of his lace canonicals, busily engaged in scouring the tall candlesticks.

One morning on their return from visiting the House of Pilate,—a curious old mansion built many years before by a resident of Seville, after a return from a pilgrimage to the Holy Land, and supposed to be a model of Pilate's palace in Jerusalem,—the girls found Mrs. Arnold radiantly happy.

"What has occurred?" Maud asked. "Has Lord Gubbins requested the honor of an introduction?"

Mrs. Arnold tossed her head in fine scorn. "A fig for Lord Gubbins. I am more faithful to my old friends than that."

"Ah! what old friend have you met in Seville?"

"Never mind. By the way, Maud, dear, that old hat of yours is shockingly shabby, take my purse and buy yourself a new one."

"But, Lily, are you wild? This is not Paris. Nobody wears hats here. I do not believe there is a milliner's shop in the city."

"Yes, there is, a new one just established, next door to the barber's-shop that Saint said might have been occupied by Rossini's Figaro. It is quite a novelty, the Spanish ladies are flocking to it and discarding their mantillas *en masse*."

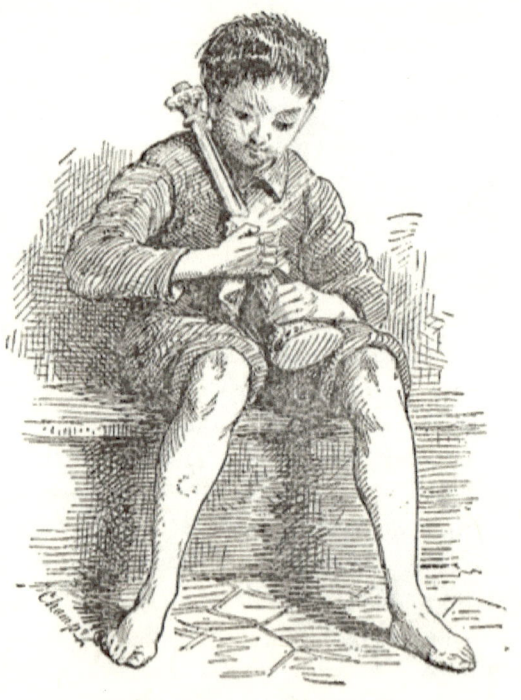

A MURILLO ALTAR BOY.

"What a pity!" said Maud; "when the national custom of draping the head and shoulders in a black-lace veil is so much more effective and artistic."

"No national custom can long resist Parisian fashion. The peaked hat of Tyrol, the folded kerchief of the Roman girl, the quaint cap of the German peasant, all give way before it."

"That is true enough, but think how stupid it will be to travel a few years hence, and find everywhere the same regulation hat and feathers. I am filled with resentment against this milliner, whoever she may be, who is trying to do away with the beautiful Andalusian mantilla."

In their next walk the girls passed the modiste's window. "Let us go in," said Barbara; "the hats are uncommonly pretty."

They were waited upon by a Spanish girl. "The proprietor was out," she explained, "but he would return presently," and she handed Maud a business card.

"So," exclaimed Maud, "the milliner is a man! Can you imagine any real live man accepting such a belittling womanish employment?"

"Girls!" cried Barbara, as she read the address on the card, "of all persons in the world, who do you imagine it is?"

THE GIRALDA.

"Not Armand Le Prince!"

"Read for yourself."

"I thought he had decided to become an artist."

"So he is, an '*artiste des modes*,' and he calls this an artistic creation."

"Girls, this is too much."

"Come with me, quick," Maud begged; "let us get away before he returns."

"Saint can go with you," replied Barbara. "I really want to buy a new hat."

"You have seven, now."

HE CALLS THIS AN ARTISTIC CREATION.

"No matter," replied Barbara, mischievously, "I want something that will attract Lord Gubbins' attention; I have paraded the whole seven before him without making the least impression. I must have something in the English style. How would this Gainsborough, lined with Vesuvius-red and tipped with heliotrope-plumes, do?"

"Atrocious, vile! Some one is coming; I fly."

As Maud and Saint vanished through one door, young Monsieur Le Prince entered by another. He seemed delighted to see Barbara, and shook hands with her very cordially. "At last!" he exclaimed in French, "we meet once more. I have looked for you everywhere."

"Your mother wrote us," Barbara replied, "that you were at Valencia."

"I travel. I establish *maisons des modes* in each city of importance which I visit. I have opened five flourishing shops. I have the honor of being the pioneer of fashion. I feel like one of the early Jesuit Fathers converting the savages. I am the missionary of good taste, the pioneer of artistic costume." He paused, and pointed with pride to the array of bonnets. "Has she seen them? Does she know that I have designed them? Ah! she could not have failed to guess that I thought only of her when I twined that wreath of forget-me-not, with this scarf of silver-shot gauze around that petit chapeau à la Marie Antoinette. Here is one of peach-blossom satin, à la Fanchon, the whole brim covered with rose-petals, and the crown, strings of point d'Alencon. In the first I thought of her as unconscious statuesque. In the second she is coquettish, and in this,"— he lifted as he spoke, an elaborate bridal-bonnet, intricately beaded with seed-pearls, — "can you not guess my aspirations when I designed this triumph of my art?"

"It is very pretty," Barbara replied, half amused and half displeased by this odd mixture of fashion and sentiment.

"One cannot design objects of art," Armand continued, "which are to become a part, so to speak, of lovely womankind, without feeling for her a profound respect and sympathy. I have studied her in all her phases until I can almost boast that I understand her. Here is a simple shade hat for the sea-shore; what more useful, more unpretending, more modestly elegant? Here is a dress hat for the opera; it is one to make the observer forget the acting, the music, or to remember it only as an accompaniment to an ethereal part of the face which this bonnet is designed to frame and to beautify. Here is a widow's bonnet. Regard, and tell me, could not the most deeply wounded heart find an asylum behind that veil, from the curious glances of an unfeeling world? Would not such mourning as that, such an admirable quality of crape, and such expensive bugles, solace the manes of the departed, and render the stricken object interesting, even fascinating, in her woe?"

Armand Le Prince paused, profoundly touched by his own eloquence.

"I fear," said Barbara, "that you have not discovered the way to please Maud."

"No?" he exclaimed, with what seemed to his listener an affectation of despair. "You told me that she worshipped beauty and admired genius, and my *chef d'œuvres* are true works of art. Advise me, kind friend, what shall I do?"

"If you want my honest advice," replied Barbara, "give up thinking of Maud, entirely. She will never care for you."

"But I admire American girls so deeply," he replied. "They have *esprit* and even learning, with a knowledge of the world, combined with an innocence which is as charming as it is wonderful. I have set my heart on marrying an American girl. Ah! Mademoiselle, if you would have the goodness to try on that white satin hat, it is possible — that it would be even more becoming to your style of beauty, than I had imagined it would be to Mademoiselle Maud."

Barbara dropped the exquisite bridal bonnet as though it had burned her fingers, and with an indignant look left the store. "And to think that I really pitied him," she said to herself, "and imagined that his feeling for Maud was something serious. Men ARE perfectly horrid!"

CHAPTER XI.

GRANADA.

THE girls did not again meet Armand Le Prince in Seville, though they passed his little shop not infrequently, and always noticed that it was an object of interest to the Andalusian senoritas. The pretty, black-eyed girls who worked in the tobacco factory, paused as they passed, the natural rose, tucked coquettishly over the left ear shining like a star in their jet-black braids, as they admired and enjoyed the less becoming coiffures displayed behind Armand's windows. Maud groaned in spirit. "They will invest in cheap hats, and the distinctive Spanish costume will be lost." As they whirled away up the mountains on their way to Granada, Maud's spirits rose. Barbara divined the reason.

"You need not congratulate yourself that you have done with Armand Le Prince, so easily," she laughed. "He will turn up in Portugal, making marmalade and *confitures*; we shall see him in paper-cap and white apron, striving to win your affection with *pates* and *gateaux*, and sugary bits of confection, as well as honeyed words of affection."

"Barb, Barb! how absurd you are!"

"Not half so absurd as Monsieur Le Prince."

"But you used to defend him; what has he done to forfeit your esteem?"

"No matter. I am very well content never to mention his name again."

"So am I, peace to his ashes, I mean his bonnets."

The next day they were in Granada. They rattled through the

PATIO DE LA ALBERCA.

town in a noisy diligence, and mounted the long hill crowned by the Alhambra. Just outside the walls stood two hotels, the Washington Irving and that of the *Torre de los Siete Suelos*, so called from one of the towers of the Alhambra, against which it backs. In spite of the name so alluring to American hearts, they took rooms at the hotel of the tower, as it offered superior inducements, and had no cause to regret their choice. Allowing but little time for rest and refreshment, they hurried to the palace, pinching their arms as they went, to make sure that they were not walking in a dream, so long had they looked forward to this visit, the crowning delight of their Spanish tour.

They entered the palace proper by an unpretentious door, and found themselves in one of the main courts, that of the Alberca, or fish-pond. The central space is occupied by a long tank, or pool, filled with darting gold-fish, which disappeared as the girls' shadows fell upon the water. The sides of this court were bordered with a hedge of myrtle and orange-trees and Japanese medlars, and the shrubbery itself is framed by long lines of elegant colonnades, richly emblazoned horse-shoe arches, resting upon delicately slender pillars. From this court they passed to the great Hall of the Ambassadors, which occupies the centre of the Tower of Comares, and is the most imposing single apartment of the palace. It was the Sultan's audience-chamber, and was well calculated to impress the visitor with his magnificence. Its lofty dome, seventy-five feet in height, like the palace of King Solomon, is " ceiled in cedar and painted with vermilion."

They stood in the central alcoved-windows which formerly held the divan of the sultan, and looked out over the balcony-railing on which Irving loved to lean and enjoy the beauty of the landscape, the Darro wedding the Xenil at the foot of the town, and the distant Vega and Sierras. Passing through the colonnades at the right of the fish-pond, they entered the celebrated Court of Lions, the flowering of the entire palace. When standing in the Hall of the Ambassadors they had been convinced that Moorish art had done its utmost to impress the stranger in this public room, with the magnificence of its monarch, but, entering the Court of Lions, they saw that a far more artistic effect had been achieved, by the grouping of a number of smaller, but elegant apartments around this charming couat.

This was the private residence of the sultan. In the centre of the marble-paved square stood the fountain from which it was named, resting on the backs of twelve heraldic Assyrian-like lions. The three salons which open upon this court, — the Hall of the Abencerrages, the Salon of the Two Sisters, and the Hall of Justice, — vie with each other in the splendor of their decoration. This suite has been called the gem of Arabian art, in Spain. They passed through the Hall of the Two Sisters, and entered the niched window, called the Boudoir of the Sultana. Here they overlooked the charming little garden of Lindaraxa, which lies enshrined like a jewel-box in the centre of the palace. Here grow cypresses, oleanders, oranges, citrons, and matted beds of rich, dark violets, whose sweet, dusky faces reminded them of the houris who once wandered here. On this garden looked also the windows of the rooms once occupied by Washington Irving. The place, to them, was full of associations with this Prince of Magicians, it would not be strange, they thought, if they saw his gentle ghost some calm midnight, flitting musingly through these deserted chambers, or seated by the blood-stained fountain-basin in the Hall of the Abencerrages, hobnobbing with the shade of the unfortunate Boabdil, and endeavoring to console him for the loss of his kingdom.

A part of this enchanted building, they were informed, had been pulled down by the Emperor Charles V., to make room for his pretentious palace, which, after all, was never completed.

They explored every nook of the palace proper, from the mysterious underground baths and whispering galleries, to the airy

CHARLES V.

FORTUNY'S MODEL.

pavilion, called the Tocador de Reina, and for days afterward found added pleasure in discovering the beauties of the isolated towers and smaller buildings in the vicinity. Irving's Tales of the Alhambra was their guide-book, they sought out with avidity every place which he had mentioned, and bought photographs with which to "inter-lay" their copies of his works.

Lord Gubbins and Mr. Featherstonhaugh were also in Granada, and often they formed but one party. Maud self-sacrificingly aided her sister to entertain his lordship, in order that Saint might stroll about with Mr. Featherstonhaugh. The Torre de la Vela was one of their favorite resorts at sunset. Here hangs the great alarm bell with the silver tongue, a bell which is kept clanging on the anniversary of the taking of Granada, for it is believed that the damsel who rings it upon that day will secure a husband within the year. When on the second of January, 1492, the city was surrendered to the Spaniards, Ferdinand and Isabella waited without with the army until they saw their banner hoisted from this tower by Cardinal Mendoza. "As the exiled and retreating Boabdil turned to cheer or chide his followers," says Bulwer, " he saw from his own watch tower, with the sun shining full upon its pure and dazzling surface, the silver cross of Spain." "What a panorama must have been visible," mused Mr. Featherstonhaugh, "from this tower upon that occasion. I think Mr. Lockhart in one of his translations of Spanish ballads has best realized the vision:

"'There was crying in Granada when the sun was going down,
  Some calling on the Trinity, some calling on Mahoun ;
  Here passed away the Koran, there in the cross was borne,
  And here was heard the Christian bell, and there the Moorish horn;
  " Te Deum laudamus " was up the Alcala sung,
  Down from the Alhambra's minarets were all the crescents flung ;
  The arms thereon of Aragon and Castile they display ;
  One king comes in in triumph, one weeping, goes away.'"

Mr. Featherstonhaugh had a fine voice, and he recited the poem with so much feeling that no one complimented him at its close. Only

Saint looked at him with moist eyes, and he seemed to feel that this was compliment enough.

Maud as usual busied herself with the artistic points of the place. To her mind the Spanish artist Fortuny had best interpreted the Alhambra, and she sought eagerly every spot where he had painted. One day there came to the hotel a rough water carrier, who said that he had served Fortuny as model; this was enough for Maud, she engaged the man as guide and made a sketch of his head; unkempt

A CHILD'S FUNERAL.

hair and bristling chin, low forehead and stolid look, there was nothing either picturesque or attractive about him, and she wondered what the great painter could have seen in him. He rewarded her pains, however, with many an anecdote of the brilliant artist, to whom he seemed fondly attached.

Mr. Featherstonhaugh seemed much interested in Maud's sketches and enjoyed looking over her portfolio of studies. He presented each of the girls with photographs of different views in the Alhambra, and Maud in return gave him a number of drawings from her sketchbook. He seemed to enjoy Barbara's bright conversation almost as much as Saint's singing, and was so impartial in his courtesy that it was difficult to tell which of the girls, if any, was now his favorite.

LOOKING OVER THE PHOTOGRAPHS.

THE GENERALIFE.

The gypsy quarter of Granada exercised a fascination over Barbara, — the horrible old crones, the lazy galliard men, sporting velvet costumes and smoking endless cigarettes, resembling the lilies of the field in immunity from toil and gorgeousness of apparel, and the bold, half naked children who clamored for money more as bandits demanding plunder than as beggars asking alms, — all interested her immensely.

"I wish I were a man," she said, "that I might study them more closely. George Borrow's accounts of adventures with this evil people, of their trickery and theft, of Gil Blas like escapades and his own wild rides through wilder regions with the gipsy Antonio, when selling the Bible made Borrow also an outlaw, — always excited my imagination. I should like to know more about them."

One day they made an excursion to the Generalife, the summer palace of the Moors, which occupies an eminence overlooking the Alhambra. They passed a little rabble of children who were strolling along in irregular procession, followed by a few elder people. It was a school, Maud thought, off for a picnic. Four boys in advance swung between them by long ribbons a gaudily ornamented raisin-box. As they approached nearer they saw that the box was uncovered, and that it held a dead baby. It was a shamefully careless funeral. The boys chatted unconcernedly as they walked, and as the girls hurried by, shocked by what they had seen, the boys set the little coffin down by the side of the road and ran after them to clamor for pennies.

They found the Generalife a garden of delight, shaded with oleander trees which seemed bouquets of rockets, and bordered with fuchsias, climbing roses and carnations, while the box grew tall and hedge-like, or was cut in fantastic forms. But the palace was only a villa, a mere mountain resort to which the sultan came for breezes of refreshing coolness when the air lay baked and still in the courts of the Alhambra

CHAPTER XII.

A BOUQUET OF LEGENDS.

THE travellers remained several weeks in Granada, and became thoroughly enthusiastic over the Moorish architecture and traditions with which the place is full.

"I do not wonder," said Barbara, "that Irving wrote so many legends; the only thing remarkable is that he could *ever* bear to stop. Why did he never write one about the beautiful palace of the Alcazar at Seville? And how could he leave out the Giralda?"

"Suppose," suggested Maud, "that we write some supplementary legends, as nearly in his style as we are able."

"Capital!" exclaimed Barbara. "Let Saint begin, and we will all follow."

"I never *could* write a composition," groaned Saint; "how absurd to imagine that I can compose a story."

"If Miss Boylston will permit me I will assist her," Mr. Featherstonhaugh gallantly volunteered; and accordingly a few days later the joint production was read in Mrs. Arnold's parlor.

Saint took the easy-chair diffidently, and explained with a voice which trembled somewhat that she was not to be held accountable for everything in the legend, as Mr. Featherstonhaugh had written "all the silly parts." The girls laughed, and Mr. Featherstonhaugh hid his face in affected embarrassment behind his portfolio of East Indian photographs.

"Now that, my dear, is hardly polite," demurred Mrs. Arnold.

"I mean," explained Saint, in some confusion, "that Mr. Feather-

TOMB OF RUNJEET SING.

stonhaugh *would* insist on the love-making, while I was opposed to anything of the sort."

The idea of that bashful and dignified young Englishman making love to any one was so ridiculous that the girls laughed again, and Mr. Featherstonhaugh, though he made no pretence of hiding his face, was evidently more genuinely embarrassed than before. To cover his annoyance, Mrs. Arnold opened the portfolio and took up a view of the "Tomb of Runjeet Sing."

"I have brought this evening," Mr. Featherstonhaugh hastened to explain, "such of my photographs of Indian architecture as present points of resemblance with that of the Alhambra. This building at Lahore, though quite modern, has much of Saracenic magnificence in its red and white mosaics of lilies and roses and in its expansive tank, without which a Moor could not imagine a palace. Other points of resemblance will be touched upon as the story progresses. Indeed, you may regard these photographs as its fitting illustrations."

There was a pause, and then Saint lifted her manuscript and read—

THE LEGEND OF THE ARCHITECT'S DAUGHTER.

Aben Cencid was one of the happiest men in Granada. And what wonder? As Master Architect of the Alhambra he had planned and superintended the execution of the intricate and gorgeous decorations which had completely satisfied his luxurious and fastidious lord, Prince Yusuf I., and had dazzled the eye and captivated the imagination of every other beholder.

In return, his Sultan had loaded him with benefits and assigned him a suite of apartments within the walls of the Alhambra near his royal person.

The Architect Cencid was a man of great talent and exquisite taste. He had travelled extensively in the Orient; and had brought back with him a camel's load of parchments, plans, and drawings, copied in the most celebrated of the temples and places of Islam. Constantinople, Tunis, Cairo, Bagdad, Damascus, Jerusalem, and Mecca were represented in his portfolios, but it was in India that he had travelled and studied most extensively. He had stood enraptured before Aladdin's Gate at Delhi, a portal so ornate that it is no wonder that it is said to be the work of the Genii of the Lamp. Its dentellated arch and banderoles, and long inscriptions in twisted strap-work characters were indelibly stamped upon his mind.

"Please Allah to send me a sovereign mighty enough to command it," he vowed to himself, "and I will make the gate of the Sultan Ala Oudin grow and blossom in another land."

Though his attention had been first turned to architecture in India there were impressions made upon his mind which influenced his career long before. His first education in Decorative Art had been received in Persia, where, the son of a shawl-weaver of Ispahan, he had watched his mother "throw the shuttle across the loom," noting with wide, observant eyes the growth of odorless roses and the weaving of gold-arabesqued arches and columns. These intricate pattern labyrinths and color harmonies blended and mingled in his brain as in the thousand shiftings of the kaleidoscope, and his busy fingers continually reproduced the fertile suggestions of his imagination. He had left Ispahan early, to study with the learned men of Bagdad and fit himself for the profession of a scribe, but copying interminable Korans was not entirely to the young man's taste, and one day he appeared in Damascus, working with gold leaf and colors as an illuminator. Then came his chance visit to India, and suddenly, standing in a court of the Pagoda of Chillambaran, there came upon him the conviction that this was the career for which he was born, to build a palace which should stand forever. But where should he find the prince who would put the means at his disposal to gratify this ambition? Saracenic magnificence was at its height in Spain, and to the Court of Granada he came. Little by little, by romantic adventure, by native

ALADDIN'S GATE.

talent, and by unpoetic drudging industry, he had worked himself up to his present resplendent position, and it was not surprising that he was a proud as well as happy man. Dearer to his pride and heart than any of his achievements or possessions, was the architect's gazelle-eyed daughter Aicha, a maiden on whose accomplishments he had spent more thought and care than on the entire decoration of the Alhambra. He was equally satisfied in the result, and now that his great life work for his sovereign was completed, he contemplated many days of reposeful charm, stretched upon his divan and lulled by Aicha's soulful voice and the soft plashing of his own fountain.

What was his disgust at the information that the Spanish King, Don Pedro the Cruel, having heard of the glories of the Alhambra, desired that his brother sovereign would lend him the clever architect, who had accomplished this miracle of beauty, to decorate his own Christian Palace at Seville. His liege lord Yusuf was anxious to be upon good terms with his powerful neighbor, and the architect had only to pack up his designs, and, selecting a corps of able assistants, to set out for Seville, hoping that he might have the good fortune to return with his head safely on his shoulders. He was met upon the frontier with an escort sent by the Christian King, and was comforting his heart with the reflection that though in the power of an unscrupulous tyrant, he was more apt to be serviceable to him alive than dead, and that he bore no riches of any kind to tempt his cupidity, when he was startled by the apparition of his favorite daughter Aicha, who had followed him at a distance upon her palfrey, and who only appeared when she knew it was too late for her to be sent back. She pleaded as her excuse that she longed to see the masterpiece with which her father would put to shame the architects of the Christian, and that she could not bear to be separated from her father. To the first argument Aben Cencid replied that he had already built for her own dwelling a kiosk overlooking the Darro, similar in style, and only inferior in size, to the Palace Bhowan, and what more exquisite casket could even the pearl of womankind desire?

Mr. Featherstonhaugh here interrupted the story to say that the allusion to the pavilions of Copal Bhowan was really an anachron-

PALACE OF COPAL BHOWAN.

ism, as the Tower of the Infantas, which might be taken as the typical home of Aicha, antedated the Indian Palace by several centuries.

"Never mind, never mind," chimed in the girls, "there is something of a resemblance. Don't spoil the story with mischievous dates."

PAGODA OF CHILLAMBARAN.

"The architect," pursued Saint, "while he trembled for his daughter's safety allowed her to continue with him, and at first his fears seemed to have been groundless, for Aben Cencid and his little suite were treated with consideration on their arrival at the palace, and were permitted to erect for themselves temporary pavilions in the royal garden. The king had either not been informed of the presence of the architect's daughter, or else he regarded the fact as of little importance, and Aicha in her latticed boudoir, in the midst of the secluded garden, was even more completely shut away from the world than in her Tower upon the Darro. The garden walls shut out all prospect of the Christian city which she had so longed to see. On an upper terrace, at the further end of the park, people employed about the palace sometimes appeared for a few moments and then vanished within the arcades, no one strolled near her window, perhaps because the king had given orders that the Moors should not be disturbed; not a sound stirred the leafy stillness except the song of the nightingales and the ripple of the brooks which watered the garden. She was quite alone, for her father and his workmen repaired every day to the palace, ornamenting its domes with many colored prismatic stalactites, and covering its walls with labyrinthine designs in Cufic strapwork, and combinations of tints which even now delight and dazzle the beholder. While its main entrance had not the grandeur of the single imposing arch of the garden gate of the Taj, there were many points in the interior that afforded a resemblance to that mausoleum "built by Titans and finished by jewellers." For the lapis lazuli, coral, turquoises, sapphires, and diamonds, he was indeed obliged to substitute corresponding colors in enamelled porcelain. He had brought with him from Granada a drove of mules and donkeys, laden with paniers filled with glazed tiles, whose metallic reflections the Moors alone knew how to fabricate, and walls and pavements as of tender-tinted gems sprinkled in intricate forms like those of snow crystals, spread a refreshing glistening coolness in the great patio, and along shady corridors. Transparent walls wrought into lace-work, fringed arches, and slender columns rose as by magic, while Aben Cencid, in the enthusiasm of his art, forgot that he was enhancing the glory of a Christian monarch, and labored to make the palace of the Alcazar worthy of the inspection of Mahomet and of Allah, the great architect who tried every man's work. The dome of the Hall of the Ambassadors, a half orange in shape, and glorious now with dusky gilding, he strove to make his masterpiece; introducing, from time to time, into the design sentences in Arabic, for he cherished a vain hope that sometime Seville might be won back by the Moors, and some Khalef of the future would read how Aben Cencid, prophet as well as architect, had dedicated the Alcazar to the heirs of Abdarrahman the Great.

Meantime Aicha, locked in her pavilion, and curtained by a luxuriant rose-tree which had been trained over her bower, gazed moodily at the beautiful garden, one of the most curious of Europe. Its parterres and fish-ponds, its labyrinths and concealed fountains, which sprayed the unwary wanderer as his foot touched a spring in the paving, its grottoes and kiosks, were all unexplored by her, — the paradise was a prison, and she wished that she had not left Granada. The only person who traversed this part of the garden was a young artist, who entered by a postern gate, of which he evidently kept the key, and who repaired to the palace each morning about an hour later than her father. He was engaged in painting the portrait of Maria Padilla, the lady love of the king, and he came and went as a privileged person. This artist, attracted by the sound of Aicha's lute, discovered the fair musician one morning, and after that came earlier each morning, and lingered for a few moments before passing to the presence of his patroness.

He had but recently returned, he told her, from pursuing his studies in Italy, where he had been instructed in the mannerisms of

GARDEN GATE OF THE TAJ.

the Byzantine school. They talked together in a mixture of broken Arabic and Spanish, and considering how little either knew of the other's language, they got along admirably. He praised her father's work with all the confidence and condescension with which a tyro will criticize or compliment the *chef d'œuvres* of a master. Aicha was pleased, and listened eagerly to all that he told her. It was fitting, he said, that the Alcazar should be finished in Moorish style, since the building was erected by the Moorish architect, Jalubi, for the great caliph, Abdarrahman. The Arabian style of decoration was not without merit, though its dentellated lace-work arches were a flat imitation of Indian workmanship, as might be seen in the courts of the palace at Tanjore.

Here again Mr. Featherstonhaugh groaned. "Your young artist, Miss Cecilia, was considerably out of his reckoning there, for the Tanjore palace is a far more modern building than the Alcazar."

" But there are the fringed arches," suggested Maud.

" Certainly, but the Hindoos adopted them along with the Mussulman rule, instead of the Saracens copying them from the Hindoos."

"Too much architecture," grumbled Barb, "do go on with the story."

"The great fault that I have to find with Moorish artists," continued Rizzi, "is that they do not represent the human face. As for myself I would rather paint the portrait of the architect's daughter than wear twice her father's honors as decorator of the Alhambra and the Alcazar." As he spoke he drew his sketchbook from a wallet and began to dash in a drawing of the fair Aicha. But the young girl gave a frightened scream and disappeared from the casement. The next day, Rizzi found her at the window, though her face was carefully shrouded with envious haic and serroual. On asking the cause of her alarm, the fair Aicha informed him that Mahomet had revealed that artists would be required at the Day of Judgment to supply souls for every representation of a human being which they had created, and failing to comply with this demand, would be obliged to forfeit their own.

"Then your solicitude, charming Aicha, was entirely on my account!" exclaimed the enraptured artist. "Know then, celestial damsel, that I gladly run this risk for the sake of possessing a faint transcript of your heavenly beauty." So saying, he prepared to begin her portrait for a second time, praying her to lay aside her disfiguring veil and allow the full moon of her effulgent countenance to beam upon him. But Aicha still objected, this time on her own account. Even if Rizzi were so mad as to draw upon himself banishment from Heaven for the sake of her portrait, and she so hard-hearted as to allow him so to peril his eternal happiness, suppose for a moment that portrait should reach the throne of The Merciful before its original, and being provided with the soul destined for the real Aicha, should pass into Paradise. What then would be her own lamentable case on being informed that there was no soul for her?

"Nay," exclaimed the infatuated artist, "you should have my soul, you have it now, and I will wander soulless to all eternity unless you vouchsafe to share it with me." He had hardly uttered this romantic avowal, when a heavy hand was laid upon his shoulder. It was that of the architect, Aben Cencid, who had returned most inopportunely from the Alcazar, and had overheard the latter part of the conversation.

"Your name, presumptuous youth?" exclaimed the sage, as, white with rage, he throttled the young man with so persuasive a grip that he was unable to pronounce a syllable.

"Slay him not, my father," cried Aicha, "he is a designer and an illuminator like thyself,—he is the talented Diego Rizzi."

"I see, indeed, that he is a designing young man," replied the architect, grimly, "and I was proceeding to illuminate the pages of his understanding, touching the etiquette to be observed toward young Moorish ladies, but it is well that you have told me both his name and his calling, for my royal master has written me to bring back with me to Granada, a Christian artist to paint some figure-pictures for his amusement, which, if they are well done, shall be hung in his own apartments."

"I thought," mused Diego, gently rubbing his twisted cervical vertebra, "that the Mohammedan religion forbade the painting of the human figure?"

"So it does," replied the astute Cencid. "So it does to the faithful, but the prophet and his followers waste no lamentations over any fate which infidel Christians may choose to bring upon themselves, and since you have already forfeited your soul many times, I see not why you should scruple to do so once more, so that my master may profit at the expense of your recklessness. I have received a signed passport from the king allowing me to journey to and from Granada as often as I choose. I purpose to repair thither upon the morrow to restore this damsel to the safe-keeping of her mother. Will you accompany us upon our journey and undertake this work for the Khalef Yusuf?"

The young artist considered for a moment. What proof had he that this was not a trap to entice him upon Moorish ground and then slay him? The sage read his doubts in his face, and, drawing a parchment from the folds of his robe, showed the demand for the services of a Christian artist signed by the hand of Yusuf the Magnificent. "This," said he, "shall be your safe conduct."

The young man still hesitated. He had already disclosed to Cencid the real motive which would take him to Granada, but with the futile prevarication common to lovers he did not wish it to appear that this was a sufficient object. "Are there," he asked, "any traces in your vaunted Alhambra of the architecture of the Orient."

Aben Cencid was at first so angry at the implied insult that for a moment he did not discern the transparency of the ruse.

"You must visit Hindostan itself," he cried, "for nowhere else, except in Granada, will you find such golden domes and jewelled minarets. Nowhere else ——"

"Stay, stay," cried Diego. "It is enough, I go."

On the morrow the little train of the architect as it wound toward Granada counted one donkey the more than it had numbered on its march toward Seville. How Diego Rizzi prospered with his painting and his wooing we leave it for *our successor to relate.*"

"Is that all?" asked Mrs. Arnold, wakened by the silence from a refreshing nap.

"Mr. Featherstonhaugh," remarked Maud, with decision, "you wrote every bit about Diego Rizzi."

"You are a young woman of remarkable discernment," replied the young Englishman. "I confess that Miss Cecilia tired of the task after the party reached Seville, and I took it up at that point."

"I was positive that Saint never could have written anything so *silly,*" Maud replied, with great satisfaction.

"But think," exclaimed Barbara, "how heavy it would have been with all that architecture if there had been no love-making in it. Talk about being crushed under the car of Juggernaut! Why we had all the temples of India piled on us."

"You should mix the light and the heavy and take a fair average," said Saint.

"Given the problem," remarked Barbara, thoughtfully, "to mix thoroughly a million tons of rock-hewn temples and a million gallons of gas — result, explosion and a general wreck."

Mr. Featherstonhaugh laughed good humoredly. "We consign the fragments," he said, "to you, Miss Barbara, for reconstruction."

Barbara, however, did not care to carry on the story of the architect's daughter. "Let us imagine," she said, "that in some way Diego carries the young woman back to Seville as his bride, and let me begin anew."

INTERIOR COURT, TANJORE.

Two days later, as they sat together in the garden of Lindaraxa, Barbara read her legend. "I have tried," she said, by way of preface, "to keep closer to Irving than you have done. You must try to imagine that he wrote the story, and that I found it while rummaging in his room over yonder. When I say *I* in the reading it is Irving that speaks, not Barbara Acheson, and so — attention, company, to —

THE LEGEND OF THE DAMASCENED KEY.

In a little tour of exploration shortly after my installation as a denizen of the Alhambra, I discovered a small postern gate leading from the garden of Lindaraxa to the ravine of the Darro, outside the walls of the Palace. It occurred to me that this gate would be a convenient mode of egress or ingress for me, communicating, as it did, almost directly with my own apartment, and I asked Tia Antonio at our next meeting if she could furnish me with the key. This worthy custodian tried all the keys upon her chatelaine, but could find none which would fit the complicated and rusty old Moorish lock.

"That must be one of the keys which Boabdil carried away with him," she said, jestingly, as she finally gave up the attempt to open the gate. "You see the path leading from the door is completely grass-grown. I cannot remember that it has ever been opened. We might have an impression taken in wax of the lock and a key made, for no modern one would fit it. See, it throws back three bolts instead of one; these old Moors knew how to work in iron. There is a chest in one of the corridors which remained unlocked for a hundred years, for no Spanish artificer was wise enough to comprehend its manner of construction. Sleep soundly, senor, you are free from intrusion from this quarter."

I thought so myself, but a few mornings thereafter, as I sat at my open window musing of the former occupants of these oriental chambers, — of the gallant Abencerrages, the fair Lindaraxa, the cruel Hassan and the unfortunate el Chico; I fancied that the gate was ajar, and as the moon rose higher in the heavens I saw that this was unmistakably the case. I did not investigate the matter at once, for I was exceedingly weary and my head was filled a drowsy humming, as of bees in a field of clover; the explanation being that I had just returned from passing the evening with the Veteran in his nest in the Torre del Vino; and he had made me taste some marvellous wine of Xeres; which, from its effects, I suspect to have been left buried in the town by the Moors themselves. I sat in a semi-conscious state for some time, my head resting upon my arm, and my arm upon the window-shelf, when suddenly I felt myself passing from the actual world into one of phantasmagoria. Lights twinkled from the windows and arcades of the palace. There was a rush of waters, and the stopped fountains gushed anew, filling the place with a water symphony, bubbling with fairy laughter, plashing in the basins, dripping with a silvery tinkle upon the pavement, and rippling away in the marble channels with a multitudinous repetition of musical sounds, alone sufficient to intoxicate the senses; so that I could fancy a composer endeavoring to reduce this wild minstrelsy to a musical formula, to become drunk with water instead of wine. I did not listen long to these sounds, for from the Court of Lions swelled a distant murmur of Oriental music, a confused mingling of drum, castanet, lute and harp. I sprang to my feet, determined to fathom the mystery, and descending a little staircase which I had discovered in the thickness of the wall of the Tower of Comares, I traversed the apartments of the Bath, and mounting a similar flight in the wall of the Tower of the Two Sisters, found myself in a little room formerly connected with the royal harem and commanding a view by means of latticed windows, both of the Court of Lions and of the interior of the Hall of the Two Sisters. The latter apartment first attracted my fascinated gaze. It was filled with fair female forms, attired in all the silken luxury of Oriental magnificence. Ladies in caftans and embroidered vests of amber, peacock blue, ruby,

MAUSOLEUM. GOLCONDA.

milky white or emerald, were seated, conversing merrily, and partaking of sweet meats, passed by slaves on gilded trays. Rich perfumes were burning in incense burners, and rose-water was sprinkled at intervals to cool the air. Presently conversation was hushed, and from a door opposite my window a young girl, shrouded in a robe of white and gold damask, was led in by two elderly females and passed around the entire company. She threw aside her disfiguring veil, and I could see that her face was very beautiful, and that she wept as though her heart would break. I sympathized with her sincerely, until I reflected that this ceremony was one of the affectations of a Moorish wedding, that no bride received her congratulations without simulating grief, and a degree of despair, which was often warranted by the events of succeeding years. The bride in question, having made the circuit of the room, seated herself in one of the alcoved windows, and a party of dancing girls in gauzy garments entered and executed a dance in the centre of the room, a delirious tornado of glancing arms, undulating bodies and whirling drapery. I turned from this wild scene and looked from the other window across the patio to the Hall of the Abencerrages. Seated about the Fountain of Lions, the musicians were filling the air with muffled drumming and strumming, and slaves were passing in and out under the fringed arches, bearing substantial dishes on which the bridegroom and his friends were to feast. I rubbed my eyes and recognized the fact that I had temporarily taken leave of my senses. This was not an ordinary dream, for I was conscious of moving about, and yet my judgment told me that what I saw and heard could only be illusory and fantastical. I determined to hasten back to my own chamber and get safely to bed before the hallucination should take on a more disagreeable form. "The Manzanilla was drugged," I reasoned to myself. "I have taken kif, hasheesh, or some narcotic, with the power of increasing mental activity a thousandfold. I will brew myself a cup of black coffee as an antidote, and endeavor to escape a permanent accession of lunacy." I remember nothing from this point until I awoke in my own bed with the sunlight across my face. "Strange dream," I said to myself, as I dressed rapidly, "I must call upon the Veteran and see how he has passed the night." And then, to reassure myself of the unreality of my experience, I went over the ground which I had traversed the night before; and found, as I expected, that the fountains were silent, the halls tenantless. Not a trace of the midnight revelry which I had seen or fancied that I had seen. I returned to my room, and leaning from my window philosophized on the force of the imagination, when again I noticed that the postern gate in the garden of Lindaraxa was ajar. "This time," I said, "there is no glamour of midnight wine or fancy to mislead me." I descended resolutely to the garden, and opened the gate. The grass around was freshly trampled, and there was a trail leading up from the ravine from the cave dwelling of the gypsies, which honeycombed the opposite cliff, that could only have been made by a numerous company. As I re-entered the gate, I saw the reason that it had not been locked. Some unknown hand had dropped the key, which I now saw gleaming in a crevice of the threshold. I had this tangible proof that the vision of the night previous was an actual experience. The key itself was a large one of curious workmanship. Composed of polished steel, it was richly damascened in gold and silver, and amongst its arabesque foliations I could distinctly trace a running line of Arabic characters.

I was considered extremely eccentric for haunting these chambers, and I kept my own counsel concerning my ghostly visitants, nothing doubting that the recital of what I had seen would confirm my neighbors in the opinion that I was mad. Long after I showed the key to an expert who easily made out the inscription:—"The king of all the earth shall open; the Khalif, the heir of Anassir, shall enter."

Next day, Maud, still in the character of Irving, followed with a—

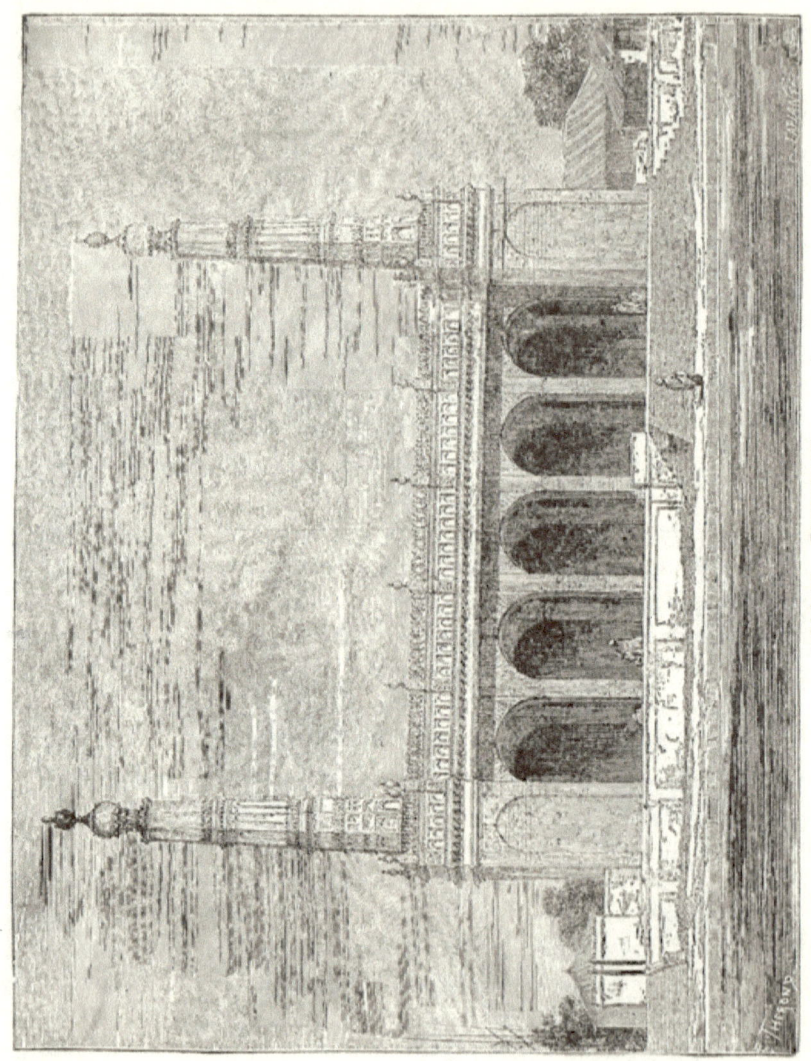

MOSQUE. TRIPLICAN.

SEQUEL TO THE LEGEND OF THE DAMASCENED KEY.

When about to return to America, having bidden adieu to my beloved Alhambra, it occurred to me that I would accept the invitation of a Jewish acquaintance of mine, a merchant residing in Tetuan in Barbary, to cross into Africa and make the acquaintance of the real Moors, the descendants of the exiles of Granada.

I found much in this strange city to interest me, much which served as a commentary on what I had observed and studied in Spain. My impressions were lively and varied, but I cannot record them here. I shall only mention one incident. I sat in my friend's bazaar, one day, a mere niche in the wall, no bigger than the show-window of an ordinary shop, and watched the motley crowd which surged and jostled its way through the narrow street. My friend explained that this was a Bedouin from the desert, that, a pirate from the Riff, one was a Nubian in the employ of a grandee, another a santo or maniac, adored as a supernatural being, when I perceived a troop of strange beggars, who received the contributions of the charitable with a certain air of distinction, as though it were a species of tribute to which they were entitled. I noticed, too, that while the santos received only copper, that silver coins were placed in the tambourine of the child who acted as receiver for this company.

"They are the descendants," my friend explained, "of Boabdil the Unfortunate. They live at Fez, but make frequent pilgrimages, in which they are occasionally joined by their entire tribe. They are on their way now to Mecca."

As he ceased speaking, a group which had especially attracted my attention, on account of its resemblance to some old Spanish altar-pieces representing the Holy Family, paused in front of my friend's shop. The group consisted of a tall and handsome Moor, rather too young to represent the Joseph of the Flight into Egypt, but, like him, leading by the halter a white mule, on which was seated a veiled

Madonna with a babe enveloped in the folds of her haic. The Moor inquired for certain commodities, and while he bargained, we entered into conversation. "Is it true," I asked, "that you are indeed of that royal race of Granada?"

The Moor replied with a dignified gesture of assent.

"And is it also true that the Moors meditate a future invasion of Spain and the reconquest of their ancient possessions? Do you hope that some day a descendant of yours will hold his court in the Hall of the Ambassadors of the Alhambra?"

He bowed gravely and with a certain dignity replied in Arabic:

"Allah will open and the Khalif will enter."

I know nothing of the language of the ancient Moors, but this was the sentence damascened upon my talismanic key; it had become indelibly impressed upon my memory. I started, and a sudden idea occurred to me.

"I see that you understand Spanish since you answer my question," I continued; "will you not kindly answer in Spanish a few questions which are not prompted by idle curiosity but by heartfelt sympathy for the wrongs of your race. It is commonly reported that the people of Morocco retain the title-deeds and maps, and even the keys of their estates across the Strait of Gibraltar, and that some day they will reclaim them when an avenger shall arise like the Sultan Selim to lead them to the slaughter of their hereditary foes."

The eye of the young man kindled, his cheek flushed.

"The map of my estates in Granada is drawn indelibly here," he replied, placing his hand upon his heart; "my title deed I keep within this scabbard," (*lightly touching his scimetar,*) "the key — I possessed it in truth once; now it is in the hands of Allah. He will open and I shall enter."

I looked at him searchingly.

"You have already entered," I said.

"It is true," he replied, simply, "and my wife has also entered.

We crossed into Spain with others of our tribe disguised as strolling gypsies. We lived for a time in the caverns of the gypsy quarter,— but one night ——"

"One night," I interrupted, "of such a date in the Alhambra, you were wedded. The bride received her guests in the Hall of the Two Sisters, and you feasted with your friends in that of the Abencerrages."

He stepped back with a look of astonishment. "You are an enchanter," he exclaimed. "You have in your possession the lost ring of Solomon with which he commanded the genii."

"No," I replied, "but I have your lost key," and I drew from an inner pocket the curiously damascened bit of metal-work which I had found at the gate. The young woman raised her veil and stared at the object with wide-eyed surprise. I improved the opportunity by a close scrutiny of her face; it was the same which I had seen in the Hall of the Two Sisters. "Madam," I said, handing her the key, "permit me to present you with this talisman; and when your husband is seated upon the throne of Spain, may his reign be as noted for wisdom and splendor as that of the magnificent Haroun al Raschid, and as admirable for piety and tolerance to alien faiths as that of the great Abdarrahman of Cordova."

"This key shall remind me of your good wishes," replied the Moor, with gentle courtesy. "If I am ever so fortunate as to regain the khalifate of my ancestors, I trust that the Alhambra may once more welcome you as its guest and mine."

We bowed at the same instant, and with such precipitancy that the turban of the Moslem softened the concussion of our skulls and whisked my spectacles from their seat. Another bow at a more measured distance, and the heir of Boabdil continued his journey toward Mecca, and I saw him no more.

CHAPTER XIII.

LISBON AND CINTRA.

THEIR stay in Granada was drawing to a close, and the evening before their departure the entire party took a promenade in the Alameda. It was their last view of the gay and picturesque Spanish people walking to and fro under the Andalusian starlight. The band played tumultuously, and the gas jets glittered. The water-carriers cried, "*Agua, agua, mas fria que la nieve!*" The children munched succarillos, or seed-cakes cut out in the shape of bulls, their horns ornamented with bits of blue ribbon. One offered Maud an Americano, which proved to be a gingerbread savage, with feathers stuck in his cranium. Maud regarded the child with surprise for a instant, and then replied, "Thank you, we Americans do not eat each other."

It was as gay to-night in the Alameda as though it were carnival time. Priests in long, shovel hats, with thong and crucifix hanging by the side of their black gowns, walked with their arms entwined with those of jauntily dressed men whose braided queues proclaimed them to be bull-fighters. Girls in white satin slippers, black-lace mantillas, enormous fans, and dresses of bright pink or blue, coquetted with theatrical-looking men in wide sombreros and cloaks. Beggar-children ran in and out, laughing shrilly, and stopping in the midst of a caper to snuffle, — "*Senorita, yo no tengo padre,*— and beg for the eighth part of a cent for the love of the mother of God.

It was their good-bye to Spain, but not to each other, for Lord Gubbins had decided to make the tour of Portugal, embarking at Oporto, for England, and they were likely to see a good deal of one another, though Mrs. Arnold had decided it would not be proper for them to travel in company. The long railway journey across the frontier was fatiguing, and gave them little of interest to repay its wearisomeness.

They spent their first day in Lisbon, quietly resting. Their first

FISH BOY OF LISBON.

sight-seeing was in the direction of mementoes of the great earthquake. The Museo del Carmen they found to be a most picturesque ruin, broken arches gave a full view of the sky, while vines entwined the pillars of the once noble church. The part of the building which still retains a roof is used as the Museum of the Archæological Society. This church, is perhaps, the only building in Lisbon which remains exactly in the same condition in which it was left by the earthquake of 1755.

One of the first spectacles which impressed the girls as characteristic of the city, was the fish market. Here were picturesque women filling their great trays from the basket of the fishermen, lifting them lightly to their heads, and setting out on a trot on their rounds through the city. There were boys, too, with purse-shaped caps, in whose capacious interior they stowed their earnings, their luncheon, and it would seem, all their extra wardrobe; and women, fishermen, and boys were all screaming together as harshly and noisily as crows in a corn-field.

Saint was especially interested in looking up data concerning the Inquisition. "Father could make a good sermon out of it," she explained; "or at least a Saturday evening lecture." At the library of National Archives she asked to be shown some of the records of this court of injustice, and when they were laid before her was disappointed to find that they were written in an antiquated, legal black letter, which, novice as she was, even in modern Portuguese, was quite beyond her power of deciphering. A young student seeing her perplexity, volunteered, with stately deference, to assist her by reading the "processos" aloud in French. Seeing that Saint took note of what he said, in English, he remarked, a shade of a smile sweeping his face, — "Here at least is something droll. It is written here in ancient Portuguese, I read it in French, and you write it again in English. Three languages are speaking at the same time, and there is no confusion of tongues."

Facing the Place Dom Pedro, one of the principal squares of the city, stands a handsome building, the Royal Theatre. It was built, they learned, upon the foundations of the ruined Palace of the Inquisition, and strange to say, the last person condemned here and burned at the stake in the square without, was executed, not as a heretic, but as a writer of merry vaudevilles, just such comedies as are now acted on the spot where he received his death sentence. Surely, even in lazy, sleepy Portugal, the world moves.

Heretics and scientists were tortured alike, for chemistry was considered a black art; but concentrated persecution fell upon the Jews, many of whom fled to the Land of the Moor, finding among the fanatic followers of the Prophet Camel-Driver more of toleration than among Christians, falsely so called.

The girls next visited the Art Gallery at Lisbon, which is made up largely of altar-pieces, etc., from despoiled convents. A most horrible collection it is. The day of doom and retribution was the most common subject, hairy, asinine devils, the central figures, and flames the background. Little else might have been expected when we reflect that the early artists had the auto-da-fes of the Inquisition before their eyes, and might at almost any time have brought their easels and camp-stools to the principal square of Lisbon and found there the actual flames of the pit.

One afternoon they rode out to Belem, a suburb of Lisbon, whose principal object of interest is the church and monastery of Sao Jeronymo. The church contains the tombs of Vasco da Gama, the discoverer of the passage to India by way of the Cape of Good Hope, Camoens the Portuguese Dante, and of Prince Sebastian the Regretted, who is thought to have been killed in Africa in a useless crusade against the Moors. Many of the Portuguese refused to be convinced of his death or to believe that the remains brought home were those of their idolized prince.

As the girls wandered in the beautiful cloister garden where the exuberant architecture of the later Gothic period seemed to be striving to eclipse the exquisite forms of the hot-house garden which it enshrined, they met Lord Gubbins and Mr. Featherstonhaugh coming out of the refectory, and together completed the tour of the monastery. At its close a guide offered to take them to the Tower of Belem, built near the mouth of the river as a fortress to protect Lisbon from the incursions of pirates. They all peered curiously into the dark oubliette into which prisoners were formerly lowered by cords, but only Barbara, Saint and Mr. Featherstonhaugh cared to climb to the windy top of the tower where were the great shields of the Order of Christ which showed from the ground only as a narrow bead of ornament. As soon as they gained one of the corner turrets and Barbara saw the water lapping the foot of the tower at such a dizzy distance below, her brain reeled, the strong wind seemed to beat her breath away, and she, clinging to the wall, groped her way down the winding staircase. Saint and Mr. Featherstonhaugh remained on the roof until the party below became quite impatient. When they came down Saint looked grave and distraught and was even more silent than usual.

LORD GUBBINS.

The next day the young gentleman who had assisted Saint in her translation of the records of the Inquisition, whose name it appeared was Jesuino de Souza y Silva, called upon them (with his mother) at their hotel, bringing an invitation for them to attend the graduating exercises of his sister's class at the Convent of Bom Succcesso. He explained politely that he saw that the young ladies were liberally educated and he thought they might be interested in seeing how Portuguese young ladies were taught. The girls accepted with great delight.

"Just fancy," exclaimed Maud, "we are going to visit the Vassar College of Portugal."

The main boast of the institution, Madame Silva explained, was the proficiency of its pupils in music and modern languages. At the appointed hour she called for them and they drove out again to Belem, where the convent was situated. They caught a glimpse of her son on a fine horse, and noticed him again after their admittance by the portress in the principal hall of the convent. He made no effort however to join them, and his call on the day before was a great concession to foreign customs, as in Portugal young gentlemen never call upon young ladies or accompany them to places of amusement unless formally betrothed. The girls noticed that the raised platform upon which the exhibition took place was separated from them by a double iron grating extending from floor to ceiling; so that they looked at the young ladies as upon rare birds enclosed in an aviary. The two gratings were so far apart that hands could just be clasped by persons reaching from either side. Had it been a menagerie, no prohibition in regard to annoying the animals with canes or umbrellas would have been necessary. The hall was decorated with specimens of needlework executed by the pupils, and by a portrait of the Pope. The papal nuncio, a venerable man in a purple silk gown, with a tiny skull-cap of corresponding color and material, just covering his tonsure, occupied an armchair directly in front of the grating. The young ladies, all of whom, with but two or three exceptions, were brunettes with rich complexions, were most unbecomingly dressed in a uniform of white, with facings of delicate blue. They entered the stage from the back and carried out the entire programme without announcement of exercises or any visible assistance from their instructors, none of whom appeared before the audience.

Various pieces of music were executed with average excellence, interspersed with recitations in different languages. Tennyson's Brook was the English selection. It was very amusing to hear the familiar words with the unfamiliar accent.

"I *charter, charter* as I go
To join the *breeming reever*,
For men may *comb* and men may go,
But I go on for *eeffer*."

The crowning glory of the programme was a "Geographical Conversation" in which all the pupils took part. This was carried on in five languages. A map of Europe hung upon an easel, and each young lady in turn would make a few remarks upon some country.

England was treated in English, the survey of Britain's greatness ending with the somewhat familiar quotation "Britannia rules the waves." A very small child came to the front and descanted on Palestine, to the great amusement of the audience, who considered her imperfect pronunciation of such hard names as Gethsemane and Golgotha as a great joke. Even the papal nuncio tittered, and the great armchair shook in sympathy with his mirth. His delight was supreme when Candida de Silva y Souza, the sister of their acquaintance repeated a panegyric on Italy in tolerably good Italian and something in the following terms:

"Rome is glorious as the cradle of the Christian religion; Padua is noted as the residence of St. Anthony, Sienna of St. Catharine, Assisi as being the birthplace of St. Francis, Milan as the bishopric of St. Ambrose, and Bologna the honored resting-place of the ashes of St. Dominick."

"I had always supposed," whispered Maud, "that Italy derived a part of its glory from the Arts, and am surprised and mortified at the ignorance in which the defective system of Vassar education has left me."

A girl of twelve next came to the front. "It is possible," whispered Madam Silva, "that you may have met this young lady in your own country as she is an American. Her name is Maria Francisca de Santo Thyrso de Parana."

"I do not recollect any one of that name," mused Mrs. Arnold. "Is she from New York?" But as she spoke the young lady in question exhibited a map of Brazil, remarking that this was her country, and this, with a few remarks on the exports of South America, served as a treatise on the western continent.

After the exercise in geography, a little girl in total eclipse behind a stupendous bouquet, addressed the nuncio, thanking his excellency for honoring the occasion with his presence, and beseeching his paternal blessing. The bouquet was handed to "Excelenzia" through the gates in the iron grating; the scholars sank upon their knees, their eyes closed demurely, and their hands clasped in devout attitudes. The pope's representative rose, (as did the audience,) and lifting two fingers, made the sign of the cross in the air, and the exercises closed with a grand choral hymn, in honor of his holiness the pope.

The names of these young ladies would alone have vouched for the devotion of their parents. That of Maria was most common, connected with different attributes of the Virgin, as Maria das Dores, (Mary of Sorrows,) Maria da Graça, Maria da Gloria, Maria Assumpcão, (pronounced Assumpcion,) Maria da Encarnacão, and such compounds as these, with the addition of a sonorous family name, was not thought sufficient, and the programme was loaded with such combinations as: —

Donna Maria das Dores Ignes Sousa Menezes; Donna Candida Stephanie Haydee Henriques dos Reis; Donna Adelia Leonilla Felicidade Santos e Silva; Donna Narcissa Eulalia Maria Annunciacão (Annunciation) Soares Vianna.

It is indeed a puzzle as to how these young ladies will be called when, in the natural course of events, they wed with young gentlemen bearing names like the following, which appear in a genuine college catalogue: —

Joao Baptista de Araujo Mirandello; José Ildefonso Placido Sebastião do Pinto; and Manoel Nepomuceno Francisco Xavier Guimarães, do Santissimo Sacramento, de Rio Janeiro, Brazil.

Madame Silva told them that they must be sure to visit Coimbra, the university town of Portugal, where her son was pursuing his collegiate studies, his presence in Lisbon at this time having been requested, in order that he might attend his sister's graduation.

Shortly after the exercises at the convent, Mrs. Arnold and the girls left Lisbon for Cintra, a place world-renowned for its natural beauties, and the favorite resort of the nobility and the wealthy. As the girls climbed the mountain-road which led to the Castle of Penha, the little town seemed to sink away from under them, and the noisy music of a band playing below was softened by the distance to a delicious murmur. The air was clear and exhilarating, and the castle on its eyrie of rocks seemed a picture rather than reality. It had a romantic, chivalric, and altogether unpractical air, utterly at variance with our work-a-day age. It could not by any stretch of the imagination, have been taken for a factory, an asylum, a railroad depot, or any other utilitarian building; it was purely and unmistakably a medieval castle, and the whole landscape appeared, as Maud said, composed to suit it, and to illustrate one of Sir Walter Scott's ballads, or a goblin story of the Rhine. The castle is occupied by Dom Fernando, the father of the present king of Portugal; he was never the reigning sovereign, but simply king consort, occupying a position analogous to that of his cousin, the lamented Prince Albert, the husband of Victoria. A German Prince, he married the Queen of Portugal and kept himself very wisely out of all govermental matters. After the death of the queen he retired to Penha Castle, and has married an American singer of some note.

"I have heard her sing in Boston," said Saint; "does it not seem odd to see her here, the wife of an ex-king?"

"Shall you call on her?" Barbara asked.

"Certainly not, I never knew her in America, and if I had I should not dare presume now. It is very good of her husband to let strangers wander about their grounds as though they were a public park."

"Shall you go to the chapel, Saint? I believe that is open to visitors."

"I think not, Maud. I am a little tired and think I will wait here in the garden until you return."

CASTLE OF PENHA DE CINTRA.

"You and Mrs. Arnold go and do the chapel," Barbara proposed, "while I wait here with Saint."

As soon as Maud and her sister were out of sight, Barbara asked, a little anxiously, "Are you feeling quite well, Saint, dear? you have not looked yourself for a day or two."

"I don't know why," Saint replied, eagerly. "I am very well."

"A little tired perhaps. I fear we may not be wise in attempting to see so much. Lord Gubbins goes straight to Oporto, while we are to make at least two stops on the way. Do you imagine that we shall meet with them again?"

"Yes, indeed. Mr. Featherstonhaugh thought it very improbable that they would immediately find passage for England, and Lord Gubbins desires to spend a few days in the vicinity of Oporto. He means to go up the river to the vineyards, to purchase a quantity of port, it is a favorite wine with the English. I believe he would rather secure a few hampers of the choicer varieties than to visit the most wonderful place in Europe."

"Mr. Featherstonhaugh does not seem as anxious to return to England as he was when we first met him. Maud and I thought then, that there was some Annie Laurie over there in whom he was particularly interested, but quite likely we were mistaken."

"No, you were quite right."

"Did he tell you so?"

"Yes, when we were alone on the roof of the Tower of Belem. He said he was deeply attached to some one to whom he had not yet proposed, and that he meant before long to 'put it to the test, and win or lose it all.'"

"Did he tell you her name?"

"No, why should he? But he asked my advice, whether he ought to mention the matter to her, when there must still be a number of years before he could ask her to be his wife."

"What did you tell him?"

"I advised him to have everything understood between them, for if she cared for him it was better that she should be sure of his affection. I told him it was not waiting but uncertainty which breaks women's hearts."

"Then what did he say?"

"He said he should most certainly act upon my advice, and I remember, too, that he promised that he would tell me the lady's name when we reached Oporto. Just before we parted he said I should know how presuming he had been, and how much above him was the being upon whom he had fixed his affections. I don't know why he wishes to tell me her name. Possibly it is because he is proud of her rank. I imagine that she must be noble."

DONKEY BOY AT CINTRA.

"Of course she is noble. Why, Saint, his secret is as easily seen through as those eye-glasses on your nose. I'll tell you who the lady is."

"Who?"

"On second thoughts I don't believe I will tell you. He evidently wants the fun of doing it himself, and I'll not be a mar-plot."

"Barbara Atchison, if you imagine,"— began Saint, the rich crimson surging to her pure brow.

"No, no; I don't imagine anything. Now don't be foolish and imagine things yourself. Time enough when we reach Oporto."

They spent several days in charming Cintra, interested quite as much in the peasants as in the scenery and historical associations of the place. Here were droll little donkey-boys tempting one to excursions to Beckford's palace or to the Cork Convent, ready to trudge contentedly behind and encourage their animals with persuasive prods of a

MAFRA.

sharp stick or by twitching their tassel-like tails. Cintra was a beautiful garden with geraniums set out in long lines along the public road, hydrangeas drooping heavy pink and white balls over the wayside walls, while superb velvety hollyhocks made hedges of rich and delicate color. Twisted cork trees, overgrown with silvery moss and an abundance of ivy and other vines twining the stone-pines and poplars, shade every lane and avenue. There was only one drawback, the beggars. They sprang up in every lovely spot, stretched beseeching hands, clamored and hobbled after them persistently. It is generally supposed that beggars are invented for the benefit of the travelling public, but the girls noticed that the Portuguese gave far more liberally than the generality of foreign tourists. One poor woman, with a number of children, opened her purse, which contained nothing but copper coins, to share it with a blind fiddler.

BEGGAR.

The monastery of Mafra, the Portuguese Escorial, faces the seashore at a distance of about fourteen miles from Cintra. Here the girls heard the most wonderful chimes to which they had ever listened, and wandered through mouldering libraries and scriptoriums. The great kitchen with its open fireplace before which whole lambs had turned upon the spit, and its capacious ovens that rivalled in size the cells of the monks; the refectory with its carved lectern where some fasting monk droned the works of the church fathers while his brethren feasted, all reminded them of Longfellow's Golden Legend, and they could easily have fancied themselves in the Convent of St. Gildas de Rhuys.

Once more upon the rail they turned their faces toward the north of Portugal. They paused only on the way to visit the Convent of Batalha and the University of Coimbra.

"Girls!" exclaimed Barbara, one fine morning as she looked from the car window, "there is the Serra Convent and the suspension bridge. We are approaching Oporto."

From the car windows they could see the Douro lined with shipping. Steaming majestically down the river was a steamship which bore the double crosses of St. George and St. Andrew.

PEASANT WOMAN AND DONKEY.

"Bound for England," said Barbara carelessly, and then she added as an after thought, "I wonder at what hotel Lord Gubbins has taken rooms?"

"It makes little difference," replied Maud. "No matter how hard we try to avoid him, we are bound to run against him sooner or later."

CHAPTER XIV.

THE NORTH OF PORTUGAL.

MAUD was wrong. None of the party ever met Lord Gubbins again. The dipping of the British ensign at the stern of the steamship as the girls passed over the suspension bridge might almost have been intended for a parting salute, for Lord Gubbins and Mr. Featherstonhaugh were on board en route for England. The latter gentleman could not have imagined a few weeks before that, when the time came for him to embark for his native land, he would be loth to go. Barbara had shrewdly guessed he had something of importance to confide to Saint, and that something did not relate to any one in England. However, the opportunity had slipped through his fingers, and Barbara and Saint looked blankly at one another when the hotel clerk informed them that he was pleased to be able to put at their service the best rooms in the house, only vacated that morning by an English milord who had just sailed for home.

As the two girls entered the smaller of the rooms, Barbara remarked crossly:

"What makes you look so smiling, Saint? One would think a load of anxiety had just been lifted from your mind."

"I feel so. I have been very unhappy ever since you hinted that perhaps—"

"No perhaps about it. I *know* to a certainty that Mr. Featherstonhaugh meant you, when he told you about that mysterious somebody in whom he was interested. I only wish for my part that he had explained himself more definitely. I can't think what possessed the man to use such ambiguous terms. Why didn't he speak up with some sort of manliness? 'Saint Boylston, I love you. Will you marry me?'"

"I am very thankful for my part that he did nothing of the kind, and that there is no chance of his ever making such a startling declaration and proposal."

"I don't know about that."

"What do you mean?"

"If his love is worth anything, oceans could not keep him from you. Besides, a trip to America is a very little thing to a man who has been out to India and back."

"Barb, you *are* crazy. He is too poor to run off on any such fool's errand."

"At all events he is not too poor to buy a postage stamp. He can at least write you. And you will see that he will."

"He does not know my address."

Barbara whistled and was silent for a moment.

"Did you never speak of home to him, of Boston, or your father?"

"I think not."

Barbara's face fell; a moment later it brightened. "I have a conviction that amounts to a sense of certainty that you will hear from him again, nevertheless." And once again Barbara was right.

Their first day in Oporto was spent upon the river. Mrs. Arnold engaged a boatman to row them up and down, and Maud filled another leaf in her sketch-book with bizarre water-side characters.

They were never tired of exploring the steep and crooked streets, of finding themselves unexpectedly in a church or market or a public square, as the case might be. Everyone seemed more active and pushing than in indolent Lisbon. Even the beggars made a business of their profession and appeared to find it a profitable one.

VIEW OF OPORTO.

"Only look!" cried Barbara, as a strange equipage approached them. "I have often heard the old rhyme, —

> 'If wishes were horses,
> Beggars might ride,'

but here comes a living exemplification of it."

It was indeed a lame beggar driving about in a queer little donkey cart, bawling ballads and accompanying himself on a discordant gui-

A LEAF FROM MAUD'S SKETCH-BOOK.

tar. The hideous little troubadour seemed in high favor and the girls saw him receive a quantity of money from the foot passengers.

The market square was bordered with the ox-carts of the peasants which brought their farm produce from the interior. They were heavy, clumsily-contrived concerns whose axles gave out ear-piercing shrieks as they rolled along. The peasants never oil them; they fancy that the shrill noise drives away the mountain wolves, and certainly, if heard in wild, solitary places this agonized cry might strike terror even to a human heart.

Our party had decided to travel a little way into the mountain region to attend a Romaria or pilgrimage fair. One of these was to be held soon at Guimarães, an historical old town north of Oporto where Affonzo Henriques, the first king of Portugal, was born, and with memories going back further still to Wamba, king of the Goths. The castle dates back to the age of fable and is now only a noble ruin.

The inn faced a square, all confusion now with the arrivals of the peasants in their *toldas* or ox-carts. The house was full, but at the sight of Mrs. Arnold's well filled purse the inn-keeper's wife surrendered her own room with its two beds, and floor as white as sand and stout arms could make it. The daughter of the house, pretty Candida, in her bright festal costume,— consisting of a dark green many-pleated petticoat, a black jacket embroidered in gold, broad white sleeves, and scarlet bodice, with a profusion of gold chains and filagree ornaments,— was a most picturesque figure.

"BEGGARS MIGHT RIDE."

She seemed fascinated by the three girls so near her own age and so different in appearance. Barbara, who had picked up a little Portuguese, greatly enjoyed chatting with her, and Candida made the effort easier by showing considerable knowledge of English which she had picked up in Oporto. Maud found her equally interesting and was wild to transfer her in all her glory to canvas.

"Would it not be delightful," Barbara suggested, "to carry home a complete suit of this brilliant costume! I mean to see if she will change for any of my finery."

Candida was delighted with the idea, and produced from her well filled chests two complete suits; one in dark blue embroidered with yellow, and the other of scarlet and black. She carried away in exchange an old silk of Barbara's which was growing rusty, and a ball dress in which she had danced last in Denver. She gazed at Maud's Japanese umbrella with such unspeakable admiration, that Maud added it also to her trophies.

The girls amused themselves by dressing up in their newly acquired property, Candida obligingly plaiting their hair and arranging gay handkerchiefs on their heads in the manner of the country. She wished also to add a gift of jewelry, but this the girls would not allow.

OX CART.

"We can easily buy ourselves some chains at the fair," said Maud, and then simultaneously to each of the girls the idea occurred that it would be great sport to attend the fête in peasant costume. If only Mrs. Arnold would consent. Besieged on all hands she finally agreed, Candida promising to walk with and take care of them, and the girls promising not to get out of sight of Mrs. Arnold and Saint.

It was to be a grand occasion — *muchas flambeaux*, Candida said, and fireworks displayed from the castle tower at night, with bands from Oporto and dancing in the public square, and on the morrow a penitential procession and high mass at the church.

An animated and almost bewildering scene was presented to

Maud and Barbara, as, unrecognizably disguised, they stole out of the inn door on the evening of the fête. The square had been turned into a bazaar, where every imaginable commodity was being bought and sold. Beyond the town, stretching up to the foot of the castle, was the encampment, ox carts in long lines changed to bedsteads, and flaring circles of camp fires where the peasants were preparing their *olhas* or national ragout. Bevies of laughing girls, dressed as they were, strolled about with intertwined arms, singing and chatting noisily to one another. Indeed, every one seemed determined to make as much noise as possible. Men shouted, boys halloed, children screamed, old women gabbled shrilly, intinerant venders called their wares, bands brayed, troubadours howled, and the donkeys, mules and oxen added their voices to the tumult. Candida led them deftly through to the goldsmith's booth and Maud invested in a chain of curious links, with a heart-shaped filagree pendant as large as her two hands, while Barbara purchased a pair of delicately wrought gold ear-rings, nearly as large as waffle irons, but of such marvellous thinness as to be neither very heavy nor expensive. As they turned from the booth a shabby ecclesiastic presented them with a silver dish filled with olive leaves.

"You must buy one of these to slip in your bosom as a talisman," whispered Candida. "They are from Wamba's olive tree in the enclosure in front of the church."

"Why then can we not pick as many as we choose without paying for them?" Maud inquired.

"No indeed," replied the girl; "during the romaria, the olive-tree is sacred, none can pick a leaf but the priest, and these have lain all night on the altar of Nossa Senhora da Oliveira. They are blessed leaves and will bring peace to your souls."

Barbara handed the beadle a coin, and slipped one of the leaves within her bodice, but Maud tossed her head scornfully, saying she would have nothing to do with such nonsense. "Why do they call it Wamba's olive-tree?" she condescended to ask.

CATHEDRAL OF GUIMARÃES, WITH WAMBA'S OLIVE TREE.

"Have you never heard?" queried Candida, in wide-eyed surprise. "Many centuries ago, in the time of the Moors, maybe,"—

"In the time of the Goths," Barbara interrupted.

"In the time of whom you will, Wamba was ploughing with a yoke of oxen where now our church stands. They were lazy beasts, and he urged them forward with a goad. Some of the elders of the land came to him and besought him to be their king. Wamba was so surprised and displeased, that he thrust his goad into the ground, and said that he would never consent until it took root and blossomed. Then Our Lady wrought a miracle, for the dead wood put out branches and leaves, blossomed with the flowers of Paradise, and showered the ground with bushels of olives. Then Wamba, seeing that it was the will of Heaven as well as of the people, left his oxen and became king. The olive-tree still stands within the railing before the church."

"How long ago was this?" asked Maud, incredulously.

"Surely I know not, but it was before the corner-stone was laid for our castle, and at the time when the blessed apostle, St. James, was fighting the infidel in Spain."

"Somewhere in the first century. Humph, your olive-tree looks remarkably green and young, considering its great age."

"Surely, why should it not? It is a miraculous plant."

A shout from the multitude announced that the display of fireworks from the castle-walls had begun. The parapet was outlined with alternate red and green lanterns, and bouquets of rockets were discharged from the tower. A set-piece, of religious character, was displayed, in which angelic forms fluttered to the earth or soared triumphantly into the starlit heavens, surrounding a central effigy, representing the assumption of the Virgin. A glory of darting flame quivered about the head of the virgin, which paused for a moment, her feet resting on a crimson globe that floated above the castle-tower, and then the strings which held the balloon, (for such it really was,) being loosened, the Virgin soared majestically skyward, and was lost from view.

The peasants screamed with delight. To the more devout and credulous it was something supernatural, and there were not wanting those who declared that the virgin herself had appeared to her favored people.

The greater part of the night was spent in hilarity and dancing.

THE CASTLE OF GUIMARÃES.

As they returned from the fireworks to the inn, they encountered a party of boys, who had spent the afternoon in a rough game of polo on their shaggy ponies, but who were not too tired for further sport. They insisted that the girls should accompany them to the dancing-pavilion.

"What is the matter with her?" one of them,—who considered himself quite irresistible, in his gala jacket, with its rows of silver clasps,—asked, as he twisted his thumb in the direction of the indignant Maud. "What is the reason that she will neither dance with me, nor speak to me?"

"She is dumb," replied Candida, who could think of no better excuse.

"But that will not hinder her dancing," persisted the youth.

"She is a cripple," explained Candida; "she sprained her ankle the other day."

"She walks remarkably fast for that," grumbled the boy. "And who is her companion, who walks so straight, and spoke to you a moment ago in such a strange outlandish gibberish?"

"She is from Vigo," replied Candida; "they are half Spanish there. Their patois is different from ours."

"Prithee, pretty maidens, whither away so fast?" said an English voice, just as Barbara and Maud had nearly reached the hotel. Barbara turned around in sheer surprise at hearing a language which she supposed no one in this region but themselves understood. The speaker was an English tourist, with a straw hat bound with an unmanly white veil. He had not, as she at first thought, penetrated her disguise, but took her for one of the peasant-girls. Mrs. Arnold and Saint appearing in sight, the stranger turned, to gaze in astonishment in his turn, at familiar costumes, and to listen to words spoken in his own language. The girls, safely in their own room, laid aside their peasant-dresses, declaring that they had had quite enough of a lark for that time.

The next day, the religious ceremonies proper, took place. A solemn Sabbath-like stillness reigned in the town, broken only by the fitful tolling of bells. Barbara rose early and attended mass with Saint, and after its close, stepped aside near the fountain, to witness the forming of the procession. A few church officials headed it, bearing the host in a silver pyx, while altar-boys in soiled lace followed with a violet velvet banner. Then came the peasants; old men with long, slant tapers; young girls with garlands and bouquets; matrons with Mater Dolorosa faces, bending over prayer-books with murmuring lips: young men walking respectfully, hat in hand. A priest followed, bearing a reliquary. "My daughters," he said to the girls, seeing that they stood aloof; "this pilgrimage is meant not alone for the poor and humble, but for the privileged as well. We are all pilgrims, and the rich have often as thorny a path to tread as the peasant. When God points out the way refuse not to walk in it."

The girls were dressed plainly in black. The priest evidently thought them well-to-do Portuguese from Oporto. Something in Barbara's heart responded to the priest's words, "I have looked so long for my path in life," she thought, "and have hoped that it might be shown me on this tour. It has not come, and the journey is almost over. What if in refusing this benevolent old man's invitation I put away my last chance of finding my path?"

A vender of relics from the Holy Land pressed toward them and offered Saint a crucifix.

"It is of olive wood, from Gethsemane," he said, "and only two *milreis*."

"Do not refuse the cross," said the priest gravely, and Saint handed the peddler the sum he asked. The procession moved on.

"Let us follow them," said Barbara; "I would like to see all the ceremonies."

She was in no way inclined to Romanism. What she had seen of the abuses and superstitions of the Catholic church in Spain had shocked and disgusted her. Barbara's faith, if she ever possessed one, must be very simple, devoid of all formalism, but it would be an earnest and living one. She was too sagacious to be deluded, but if the priest had a message of truth to communicate, she was broad enough to accept it and wise enough to winnow the wheat from the chaff. Even now her quick judgment was on the alert, suspicious of fraud, but her heart was in a susceptible mood. Some spiritual influence beyond her own inclination seemed to draw her on. They followed to a spot where a temporary *via crucis* had been constructed, with fifteen stations or wayside altars, before each of which the pilgrims paused and offered prayer. The last shrine was placed on a roomy esplanade provided with rough benches facing a pulpit which the priest, who had spoken to them, ascended, and, when all had taken seats began a sermon. Much of it Barbara could not understand, but she felt the magnetism of the listening, earnest people. She saw that the preacher was eloquent, for his audience wept frequently, and now and then she understood a distinctly uttered phrase, or even comprehended the drift of an entire sentence.

While others sobbed their repentance or sorrow, care or pain, Barbara murmured only

> "O, that the mist which veileth my To come
> Would so dissolve and yield unto my eyes
> A worthy path! I'd count not wearisome
> Long toil, nor enterprise."

"Maud goes back," she thought, "confirmed in her art work, asking no other. To Saint, though she has her music, there is coming some time I am sure the greatest joy which can come into any woman's life — the love of a truly noble soul. But I have nothing; an aimless life is hardly worth the living."

The priest repeated his text — "Sir, we would see Jesus!" Of what followed she only understood broken sentences, somewhat in this wise: "You have all paths to choose — the path of sin, the path of pleasure, of earthly wisdom, of honor and the delight of the world. But *one* path leads to Jesus, the path of renunciation and self-denial. You would see Jesus? He is walking to and fro among you. His hand is laid upon yours; he would lead you to himself. In every act of self-sacrifice, of unselfish love that is done in the world, in every faithful performance of duty we find the heavenly walk.

"You would see Jesus? Then you need not inquire the way, your feet are already in it. Press on, moulding your life after His; walking in his footsteps; and all the way you shall hear the flutter of his garment going on before. You shall walk in his shadow, which

GATEWAY.

is perfect light, and at the end — which is but the beginning, then for ever — you shall see — Jesus."

Was it the miraculous work of the crisped olive leaf which lay over Barbara's heart or of an influence more truly divine? A glamour as of a holy radiance seemed shed upon castle and hillside upon the quaint town, and an ancient gateway through which the sunrise shone till it seemed to her like the gate of Heaven, upon the face of the almost inspired preacher and his kneeling people. This was what she had longed and yearned for so long, not knowing what she sought. She, too, would see Jesus. Her feet were in the path and all its onward way was marked by him. She knelt as in a trance and the peace of God entered her soul.

CHAPTER XV.

A GLIMPSE AT AFRICA.

ON their return to Oporto, Mrs. Arnold found a letter awaiting her from her husband. He stated that the United States frigate on which he was a lieutenant, was ordered to Gibraltar, and that if she could come immediately to that port he could meet her there. Fortunately an English steamer bound for Gibraltar had just put into Oporto, and Mrs. Arnold and the girls took passage at once.

Arriving at the rock, which British engineering has changed into the most invulnerable fortress in the world, Mrs. Arnold was delighted to see the stars and stripes hoisted in the harbor, and as they were rowed to shore she recognized in the crowd of Jews, Moors, Spaniards, and English, who thronged the wharf, a well-known form in the uniform of the United States Navy.

After the party had inspected the galleries in the Rock, had climbed to the old Moorish castle, and had enjoyed the cosmopolitan sights of the market, and review of the British soldiery, in their dazzling white helmets and brilliant scarlet uniforms; they met in the drawing-room of the Royal Hotel, for what the lieutenant called a council of war.

"My ship will be detained here," he explained, "until we receive advices from America. The girls can not set out for America until the arrival of some chance steamer or one of the regular fruit-line from Malaga. None of these are expected until next week. Now the question arises, how shall we spend the intervening time? It seems to me that nothing could be more interesting than a trip across to Tangier. I can easily obtain leave of absence for a couple of

ROCK OF GIBRALTAR.

days, and if the place is anything like Algiers it is well worth visiting."

Mrs. Arnold demurred. They were all "Turks" over there, and she did not care to risk her life among them.

SKETCH IN GIBRALTAR.

"Not Turks, Lily, but Moors," Lieutenant Arnold corrected. "It is a time of peace, and I am sure a little lady who has knocked about all sorts of harum scarum places in Spain and Portugal, ought not to be afraid, now that she has a representative of the United States Navy to protect her."

Mrs. Arnold at length gave a grudging consent, and the party embarked on the tiny Jackal, for Africa.

"This is a fitting ending for our tour," exclaimed Maud. "A bit of real Orient; bazaars, and mosques, harems and caravans. Oh, it is just —

"Too quite too far more than most awfully delicious," suggested Saint.

A near view of Tangier showed more of filth than of magnificence. Narrow alleys in place of streets, noisome smells, and fierce, wicked faces scowling at them from under turban and fez. And yet there was compensation for much inconvenience in the strange sights about them, — bazaars that reminded Maud of Fortuny's pictures, in their display of rich colors, tiled minarets and towers flashing back the sunshine; palm-trees drooping over white walls, and stranger human types. There were light-complexioned Moors with haughty profiles, richly-clad. Jetty negroes, nearly naked, bearing baskets of tropical fruits; wild Bedouins from the desert, carrying long rifles, women shrouded in the haic, which only permitted one eye to be seen; cringing, shabby Jews, and idiotic or lunatic *santos*. These last are regarded as sacred by the Moors, who believe that God has withdrawn their souls to Heaven. A santo crouched beside the door of the hotel as they entered, and spat viciously at Mrs. Arnold, who chanced to step upon his tatters. The lieutenant thoughtlessly threatened the man, bidding him be more civil. Whereupon the santo rose slowly and cursed him in Arabic. A son of the hotel-keeper, who chanced to be near, looked frightened. "You have done a very impolitic thing, my master," he said; "this santo is in great repute with the populace, and has almost unlimited influence over the Pasha of Tangier."

"What did he say just now?" Mrs. Arnold asked.

"He said that it was one thing for Christian dogs to come to a country where you were not desired, and another to get away from it safely."

BAZAAR IN TUNIS.

"There, Edmund!" exclaimed Mrs. Arnold; "did I not say that this was a dangerous place? The Jackal has not left yet, let us go on board immediately."

"Nonsense," replied her husband, "the vagabond cannot hurt us, It would be absurd to come to Africa only to leave it in half an hour," and entering the hotel, he took rooms and ordered dinner. After dinner they took a walk to the Soc, or market-place without the walls. Here a caravan had just arrived from Timbuctoo, by the way of the desert, and the girls watched the unlading of the camels with much interest. They returned by way of the bazaars, and the lieutenant purchased trinkets for all; silver bangles for Barbara, a scarf, shot with gold thread, for Maud, and a small prayer-rug, of Tunisian manufacture, for Saint. A Moorish arch in the gay pattern, designated the end which

A SANTO.

was always pointed toward Mecca, and the space within was worn nearly threadbare by the knees of the faithful.

They peeped inside the door of a mosque, and visited the house formerly occupied as a studio by the French artist, Henri Regnault. Here they heard a French voice conversing with the Jewess who was doing laundry work in the beautifully arched court. Barbara grasped Maud's hand and the two girls turned and fled. The voice was unmistakably that of Armand Le Prince.

"To think that we should find him here of all places in the world!" said Barbara.

"It is not so very strange," replied Saint; "we left him in Seville. It is quite natural that he should continue his tour southward."

"He has not discovered us so far," remarked Maud; "let us hope that we may escape him."

The next morning as the girls entered the breakfast-room they found Monsieur Le Prince in animated conversation with Lieutenant and Mrs. Arnold.

"Come here, Maud," cried the latter, "and help us congratulate Monsieur Le Prince on his marriage."

It was really true. Armand had married a Spanish lady and had left his bride in Gibraltar, while he visited Tangier to see if he could establish a bazaar of bonnets for Moorish ladies. They chatted very pleasantly during the meal and the girls confessed afterwards that Armand as a married man was far more interesting than as a bachelor. He had not met with success in disposing of his wares. The Moorish ladies rarely appear on the streets, and it was impossible for him to enter their houses to show them his tempting bonnets. Moorish husbands and fathers passed him by; they looked with no favor on Christian schemes of money-making. It was a vile country, and he had determined to quit it that very day.

"I don't know but we have seen enough of it also," remarked the lieutenant, "unless you young ladies would like a trip per caravan across the Sahara."

"Oh! do let us go, Edmund," pleaded Mrs. Arnold. "That horrible Santo is back at his post, and looked at me in such an evil way this morning that I am sure he means mischief."

The lieutenant saw that his wife was really uneasy, and although regarding her fears as childish, he was quite willing to humor her. No one cared to remain longer but Maud, who was anxious to make

DOOR OF MOSQUE OF BOU-MÉDINA.

some studies in color. The inn-keeper was appealed to for information as to the departure of the boats.

He shrugged his shoulders with an expressive wave of the hands. "When Allah wills."

"What do you mean? Have they no regular times of coming and going?"

"Certainly; without doubt the Jackal might be expected on the morrow, but it would not be permitted to land; the port was in quarantine."

"In quarantine! Is there fever in town?"

"No, it was never more healthy. The authorities often announce the place in quarantine for months together, for reasons of their own which none can fathom."

"But this is absurd; it is unendurable," rebelled the lieutenant. "I will see the pasha."

"It will be useless. It is he who has issued the decree at the advice of the Santo."

"The Santo! I told you so. I told you so," moaned Mrs. Arnold.

"And I am to be separated an indefinite eternity from my wife!" exclaimed Armand Le Prince.

"Do see the American consul," suggested Maud.

"The very thing," replied the lieutenant. "I always supposed that Decatur put an end to the capture of American citizens by Barbary corsairs. The thing is an insult to the flag; it is not to be borne. Moreover, I am liable to court-martial for overstaying my leave of absence."

Even Maud had suddenly lost all desire to make any sketches, and was as anxious to get away as any of the others.

The lieutenant returned from a protracted tour of all the consulates, dispirited, weary and unsuccessful. No one could do anything, and he was advised on every hand to wait patiently. The embargo would not probably last more than a week or two, and meantime he might make a trip to Tetuan or even Fez.

"Could we not bribe some of the boatmen to take us across the Straits in one of those feluccas with the rakish latteen sails?" asked Mrs. Arnold.

"I have thought of that," replied the lieutenant, "but the enterprise would be a hazardous one, and if we failed in getting off or were overtaken we would probably be imprisoned. I do not like to risk it."

"As well one danger as another," said Maud. "I am confident that annoyance is not all which the Santo has planned for us. He will, I fear, excite the populace against us and cause us to be massacred."

Saint shuddered, but Barbara replied cheerfully, for a conviction that they were all in God's hands made her brave:

"I do not think they would dare do anything like that within sight of one of our own war-ships and in the presence of the foreign legations. The delay *is* provoking, but Maud at least can profit by it. If Mrs. Arnold would feel safer perhaps we can prevail upon our consul to take us into his own household. I am positive the quarantine cannot last long; it puts the Moors themselves to too much inconvenience."

Armand Le Prince who had been silent for a long time, smote upon his forehead.

"I have an idea!"

CHAPTER XVI.

HOME AGAIN.

ARMAND'S idea was a good one, but it could never have been carried out without the co-operation of the girls.

"European ladies," he said," are frequently allowed to call on the harem of the pasha, — where no man would be admitted. If you will call on these ladies, I think our liberation could be effected."

"I am afraid they would care very little for our entreaties," replied Saint.

"Nothing, doubtless. You shall not entreat; we will leave that to them."

"What do you mean?"

"Simply this, you shall each of you carry a couple of bandboxes, they contain the most ravishing specimens of my talent, present these to the ladies. There will not be enough to go around, good! Tell them that more will be forwarded from Gibraltar as soon as the quarantine is raised. Ah! that old pasha, I pity him, he will have no peace. When the Jackal returns, we will all stand upon the deck."

"The experiment is at least worth trying," remarked the lieutenant. "We will see whether Monsieur Le Prince has rightly estimated the caprices of the female mind."

The lieutenant and Antonio, the son of the hotel-keeper, accompanied Mrs. Arnold and the girls to the audience-room of the pasha, where the whole party salamed humbly, while Antonio interpreted the desire of the ladies to visit the pasha's harem. In order to impress the pasha with the dignity of his guests, Antonio unscrupulously informed him that the lieutenant was the Pasha of New York, and that the girls were the daughters of General Washington. The pasha waved the gentlemen to seats upon the divan, and clapped his hands for a little Nubian to lead the ladies to the apartments of the women. "If Washington is the father of his country," said Maud, afterward, "I suppose that in a figurative sense, Antonio was right, and we really are daughters of Washington."

The Nubian led them to a beautiful interior court where the pasha's ladies were assembled in gorgeous Moorish costumes. Their guide explained, as he had been told by Antonio, that the foreign ladies had brought them some presents, and Maud proceeded to open the bandboxes. "Where are your scruples now?" Barbara asked, mischievously, "about abolishing the national costume of a country?" How can you bear to substitute Parisian hats for those lovely spangled gauze veils?"

Maud pretended not to hear her, and herself put on the marvellous bridal hat, which Armand had originally designed for her, in order to show the ladies the proper way to wear it. A wrinkled crone of some sixty winters, the pasha's senior wife, came forward and claimed the first gift as due to her pre-eminent position. Mrs. Arnold could not forbear a little grimace as the orange-blossoms were arranged above her frosty locks. The "chapeau ingenue," or of unconscious innocence, was fitted to the head of an uncommonly fat woman of forty.

"She looks like a squaw," murmured Barbara.

The coquettish flirtation hat was next jauntily pinned on the woolly chignon of a belle from the Soudan, and nothing remained but the widow's cap, "douleur extreme" for a really pretty girl of eighteen. Thekodalis, the pasha's favorite and latest wife, a lovely creature of sixteen, had nothing. A frown contracted her beautiful brows, and she retired to an alcove, pouting sulkily. Then the Nubian guide repeated what Antonio had told him. More bonnets would be sent when the quarantine was raised. More wives came in from the garden and looked longingly at the presents, while the fortunate ladies hastened to regale their benefactors with tiny cups of tea, siropy sweet and flavored with verbena.

"To think," laughed Saint, on their return to the hotel, "that after all that happened at Seville, Maud should really be on good terms with Armand Le Prince, and that I should see her actually assisting him in the disposal of the bonnets which she professed so greatly to detest."

"Both Armand and the bonnets are very well in their place," replied Maud; "and that place seems to be the present emergency. If they save our lives now, I shall be willing to recognize Armand as the artist he claims to be."

The next day, the longed for announcement was brought to them that the embargo was at an end. The Pasha of New York was at liberty to leave with his harem, at his pleasure. The message was accompanied by a gift of Moorish silken stuffs, which were forced upon the unwilling Armand, and the request that more bonnets might be sent to the Pasha of Tangier.

"With those bonnets," said Saint, gaily, "will surely come the desire of gadding abroad to show them. To us is due the first breaking down of Moorish tyranny to women."

At Gibraltar a steamer was found ready to sail for America. The girls were placed under the care of the captain's wife, and Lieutenant and Mrs. Arnold, and Armand Le Prince and his bride, accompanied them on board. Armand brought three bandboxes containing triumphs of his art, which he begged the girls to accept, in testimony of his "respect profound, his gratitude sincere, and his friendship eternal."

His pretty wife added her protestations of regard, and all waved their handkerchiefs enthusiastically from the wharf, as the girls started on their homeward voyage.

The trip was as uneventful as most ocean transits. The most interesting personage on board, to the girls, was a Chinese boy, the servant of a gentleman who had resided a number of years in China.

He always addressed the boy in pigeon English, a strange mongrel patois that was often extremely amusing. He was bringing home a great many curios,—delicate sets of porcelain, exquisitely

HOME AT LAST.

embroidered silks, carved ivories, lacquer boxes and dragon vases. As he approached New York he became quite nervous at the thought of the custom-house, and at the enormous duty which might be charged on these articles. It struck him at last that if they were passed through as the property of the young Chinaman, the officers might be more moderate in their estimate. He called his servant to him and proceeded to place all the valuable articles in a single chest. This he locked, handing Kong the key with the injunction—

"Kong! s'pose some man talkee, 'who that chest b'longee?' Say, 'that chest b'longee my!' Sabe?"

Kong appeared to understand, but Barbara, who had overheard the conversation, was much shocked.

"That gentleman will regret the day he taught his servant to lie," she said to the other girls.

This proved to be the case sooner than was expected, for as soon as the officers had finished their examination and had returned the key to Kong, he shouldered the chest, and from that moment neither it nor he were seen again.

It was surmised that he had taken refuge in some of the Chinese laundries, but he evaded all pursuit. The gentleman's property was irrecoverably lost. Evidently he had understood, far too literally for his master's satisfaction, " that chest b'longee *my*."

The girls received an enthusiastic welcome from their classmates at Vassar, who arranged a little spread in their honor, at which a song originally written to the Harvard annex was so sung as to apply to them —

"These are the undergraduates
Of 1883,
The prettiest undergraduates
That ever you did see.

In Spanish and in Calculus,
And in Hindostanee,
Their learning is quite fabulous,
As well as Portugee.

The verb abstruse, *amo, amas*,
In Latin and Chinee,
In every tongue each clever lass
Can conjugate freelee.

Music is represented by
Its patroness, Saint C.,
In painting Maud will soon surpass
Raphael or Da Vinci.

> From every European State,
>   From South Amerikee,
> From Popocatapetl, and
>   From Asia and Fiji.
>
> These pretty modern Eves have come
>   This Class of '83,
> To pluck the golden apples from
>   The one forbidden tree."

"You have not mentioned Barbara," said Saint. "Barb, what do you call yourself?"

"The great American appreciator," replied Barbara, laughing.

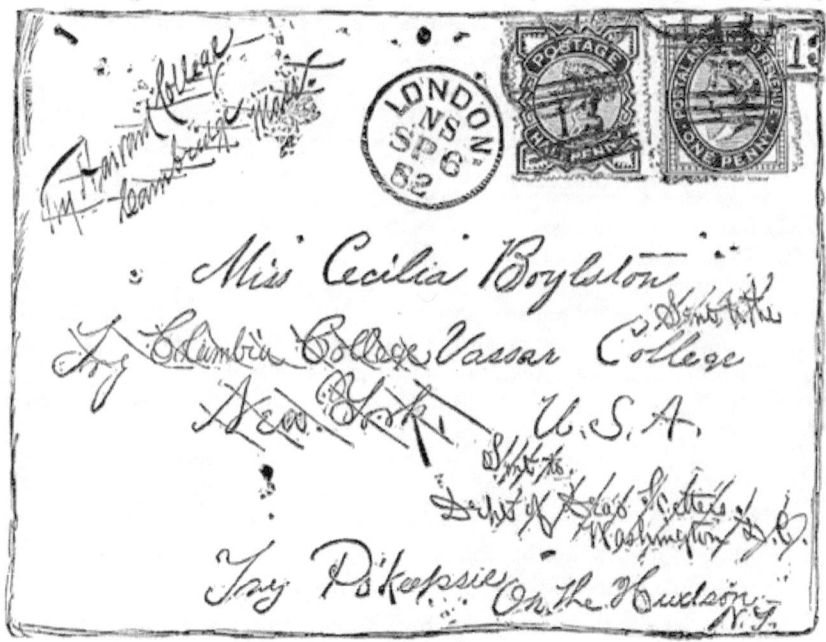

One day Saint received a letter strangely addressed and much crossed and recrossed by the random suggestions of postmasters by whom it had been bandied about. The envelope was nearly worn out and presented an appearance something like the above.

Opened, the letter was found to read as follows: —

LONDON, Sept. 5.

MY DEAR MISS BOYLSTON:

To my great regret, our departure for England was precipitated by the unexpected arrival at Oporto of just the steamer which his Lordship desired to take. So sudden was our leaving that I had not time to do more than to leave the hurried scrawl with our hotel clerk with instructions to find you if possible on your arrival, and deliver it to you.

"But I never received anything," exclaimed Saint.

"Certainly not," replied Maud. "Who ever heard of a hotel clerk putting himself out to serve any one, especially if he was paid beforehand?"

That note very inadequately expressed my reluctance at leaving the country before having at least one more interview with you. Our only means of intercourse for the present is through the medium of correspondence; and difficult as it is for me to express myself in this manner, I shall endeavor so to do, should this letter be so happy as to reach you, and you so kind as to deign a reply.

I have much to say, and something of what I would have said I believe you have already guessed. I am sure, from the advice you gave me at Belem, that you recognized the portrait which I endeavored to sketch for you, and no one can be in a better position than yourself to give advice in the matter. If you still think my case a hopeful one, will you not drop me a line at the enclosed address, and I will remain ever, your obliged servant,

FEATHERSTONHAUGH.

"Now I call that unexampled impertinence," exclaimed Saint. "The idea of his imagining that I advised him to persevere because I thought he meant me! It is simply insulting."

"No, not so bad as that," replied Maud, critically; "he seems to me to be absurdly cautious, however. Do you notice that he does not commit himself even now? How shall you answer the letter?"

"I shall not answer it at all. He can imagine, if he chooses, that it never reached me."

"Now, Saint," pleaded Barbara, "that is really too bad. Father writes that if I maintain a good position in my class this year he will take me to England himself next summer. He intends to apply for a leave of absence, and hunt up some English relatives of ours. If we go—"

"If you go you will probably see Mr. Featherstonhaugh," interrupted Saint, "but I do not expect ever to see him again." There was no regret in her voice as she said this, and she continued calmly, "All has ended very well."

But Barbara shook her head and smiled. "If I can help it," she said, "this is not

THE END."

www.ingramcontent.com/pod-product-compliance
Lightning Source LLC
Chambersburg PA
CBHW021827230426
43669CB00008B/887